FOOTBALL: THE VIOLENT CHESS MATCH

A Fan's Guide to Strategy

TOM FLORES AND BOB O'CONNOR

MASTERS PRESS

A Division of Howard W. Sams & Co.

Published by Masters Press

(A Division of Howard W. Sams & Co.)

2647 Waterfront Pkwy. E. Drive, Suite 300

Indianapolis, IN 46214

Published 1994

Printed in the United States of America

Library of Congress Cataloging-in-Publication Data

Flores, Tom.

    Football: the violent chess match /Tom Flores and Bob O'Connor.
         p.   cm.
    ISBN: 1-57028-001-0 : $12.95
    1. Football. I. O'Connor, Robert 1932-   . II. Title.

GV951.F56   1994   94-22144
796.332--dc20   CIP

Credits:

Cover design by Julie Biddle
Front cover photo by Corky Trewin, courtesy of the Seattle Seahawks
Diagrams by Julie Biddle and Jason Farmer
Edited by H.W. Kondras and Heather Seal
Production assistance provided by Kelli Ternet

CONTENTS

DEDICATION

We dedicate this book to Hank Stram, former head coach of the Kansas City Chiefs and one of the truly outstanding coaches of all time. Hank was Coach of the Year four times and a Super Bowl winner. He won every big game there was to win. No one has contributed more to this great game than Hank. From the sidelines or from the broadcast booth, his insight and intensity as well as his love of the game shine through and stimulate us all. We hope that he will soon be accorded the honor of election into the Pro Football Hall of Fame – a recognition which he justly deserves.

PREFACE

Football is considered to be the ideal spectator sport. It has more action per play than any other sport—22 men, each with his own assignment on every play. It allows for the ultimate in game strategy, because after each play, the teams can regroup and change tactics. The pauses between downs give the spectators time to analyze, comment, and make predictions on the next play. We can really get involved in the game of football.

After a recent New Year's Day of watching four football games, my brother's wife said to him, "You beast. You love football more than me."

"Yes, I know dear," he replied, "but I love you more than basketball."

Whether it is the high school, college, or professional game—it is exciting. We always have a reason to root for somebody—our home team, our favorite team, the underdog, or the players that we know.

Almost everyone gets some enjoyment out of watching a football game. Sometimes it is because his or her alma mater is playing. Sometimes it is the "big game" of the week. Sometimes it is just an enjoyable pastime to enjoy while sipping a beer or Pepsi. But the game is always more enjoyable if you know something extra about it. If you know one of the players, if your favorite team is playing, or if you understand the strategy involved in the situation—your interest becomes more intense.

A recent newspaper survey asked the average "fan on the street" what a nickel defense was. Only one out of 20 fans were able to answer correctly. Yet the nickel defense is an integral part of professional football tactics. Perhaps the "color men" who are hired to give insights into the game have not given as clear a picture as is needed to help us understand the changing complexities of the modern game of football.

In this book, we will look at the game in its simple form so that beginners will be able to understand it better. However, we will also look at the more advanced intricacies of the game so that the real football aficionado can gain more from the game.

We hope that you will enjoy reading the book as much as we have enjoyed writing it. We also hope that you will be able to enjoy every game even more because of your increased insight into the sport. The more we each learn as coaches or fans, the more we seem to get caught up in football fever each year.

A toast to all football incurables everywhere!

Tom Flores and Bob O'Connor

Hank Stram

FOREWORD

When Tom and Bob came up with the title *The Violent Chess Match*, I was amazed at how they had captured the essence of the game in the title. Certainly for coaches, it is a chess match.

Every weekend during the season, coaches pour over the scouting reports and watch films of their upcoming opponents. Once they know what the opponents do, how they think, and which players will be in uniform, they begin to plot their offensive, defensive, and kicking game strategies. They look for how they can create mismatches and put their better players against the weaker players of their opponents. It's "me against the other coach." It's our team against his. How can we load the dice so that the odds of winning are in our favor?

Football is a very complex game. That's why it holds the fascination of Americans and is rapidly spreading to Europe and Japan. It's a war – Napoleon against Wellington, MacArthur against Tojo, Grant against Lee. It's a game of head and heart, of intelligence and courage. Fans see the raw courage on the field but often miss the intelligence being used by the quarterbacks calling the plays and reading the defenses. They miss the blocking calls of the offensive linemen. This book gives real insight into the underlying elements of the game from the coaches' point of view.

But more than the strategy, I particularly enjoyed reading about some of the great players of the game who contributed their thoughts to the book. Otto Graham, Mel Hein and Jim Otto are certainly all time pros whose thoughts on the game will delight you. Then there are two of Tom's current players, Rick Mirer and Cortez Kennedy who show a continuity of thinking among the great players of this game.

The insights found in this book will give you an understanding and appreciation which will increase your joy in watching football – America's greatest game.

Hank Stram

Photo Credits

Michael Bates

1
FOOTBALL IS A SPECIAL GAME

The great composer Franz Liszt once said, "Every theater is a lunatic asylum and opera is the ward for the incurables." The same might be said about the aficionados of football. Whether they be part of the Monday Night millions, the Pop Warner coaches, or the players and coaches at the higher levels—for whatever reason, people think football is fun.

It's fun to play, it's fun to coach, and it's fun to watch. Regardless of the degree of involvement, most of us have a gut involvement in the game. Whether I associate myself with the Seahawks or the Huskies, the Bengals or the Bruins, the Crimsons or the Cardinals, it's my team, win or tie!

Football probably tests the raw physical courage of a man more than any other sport. Robert Lewis Stevenson, the author of *Treasure Island*, once said, "Courage is the footstool of other virtues."

In nearly all cultures, the badge of courage separates the desirable young men from the rest of the pack. Whether it is the killing of a lion by a young African, the lonely battle against the elements by a young American Indian in his initiation to the circle of braves, or the tackling of an opponent by a young football player, courage is exhibited. Every society recognizes courage and applauds it.

If the psychologist Alfred Adler is right, we all have a drive for power — a drive to overcome our feelings of inferiority. This could certainly explain the joy felt in making an aggressive block or tackle, throwing or catching a pass, kicking a field goal or blocking a punt. It might also explain the fascination of the coaches in designing an offense or defense, or in molding a group of young people into an effective team.

We see that drive for power in the building of businesses, in the desire to move up in the political circles that drive our country, even in the relationships of men and women and adults and children. It is everywhere. Why do we laugh at the comedian who slips on a banana peel? Because we are better than he is!

Part of the fascination with football is that it is a collision sport. If my team's wide receiver goes across the middle, catches a pass between the linebackers, and survives the hit by the strong safety, I am ecstatic. I have won. If my defensive line twists its tackles and breaks free to sack the quarterback, I have won. All of us on the winning side — the coaches, players, and fans — feel the exaltation of the hit and the

Coaching legend Vince Lobardi

win. We are all sensing the satisfaction of our drives for power and success. Probably no people on earth want to win as much as the Americans. We are accustomed to winning. The Revolutionary War, the Industrial Revolution, and the World Wars have provided a tradition of victory that is part of our national fabric.

But love is part of the makeup of football as well. When thirty or forty young people and coaches go through the preseason practices, or "hell weeks," together, a feeling of mutual respect and comradeship develops. When you see the defensive team huddled and holding hands, you are witnessing a feeling of family. Did Vince Lombardi care for his players? You bet he did!

The psychological drives we all experience are magnified in the football arena. Boys and men who have worked together for nine months in the weight room, who have sweated together during the daily practices, who have experienced the exhilaration of winning and the sting of defeat, have developed a brotherhood that transcends the color of race or the belief system of a religion. They are brothers, and the fans join in that brotherhood.

Fans of professional, college, or high school football also develop a sense of oneness with the team. Simple acts such as purchasing expensive season tickets, making generous donations to high schools or colleges and setting aside every weekend (and Monday night) during the season to cheer on their favorites help fans develop a bond with the participants — after all, they are making sacrifices too.

Dedicated fans usually know about the players, but they don't always understand the intricacies of the game. The more fans know about an activity, however, the more enjoyment they can get from it. In this book, we will take readers beyond the superficial knowledge of the players and teams and offer a glimpse into the game itself.

Most fans merely want to see more passes thrown. The sophisticated fan understands the game is much more complicated than that. Victory can be achieved in many ways. A coach might know, after watching 30 hours of game films, that his players are overmatched in the passing game or on defense. He might know that his best receiver has a sprained finger. As a result, he might try to win with defense, with the kicking game, or with the run. Understanding the week-to-week challenges is only one factor in the coach's decisions relating to a game plan. There is so much more than the average fan sees.

This book is organized to explain the following topics:

- What is the special fascination with football? Why are there so many devoted coaches, players and fans of the game?

- What are the theories behind the game? How can a team best win? What type of offense and defense are most appropriate? What are the advantages and disadvantages of each? This is the area of preseason planning. It is a major consideration in drafting players for the pro teams and in recruiting for college teams.

- Strategy—the week-to-week adjustments in the game plan relating to how the coach can find mismatches and opportunities for success.

- Tactics—the immediate adjustments that must be made to what the opponent is doing or to factors such as injuries.

- Finally, and perhaps most importantly, we will inform fans how to watch the game to get more enjoyment from it.

We want you to understand and enjoy this "violent chess match" — our great American game.

2
Why They Play The Game

We start any recreation because we enjoy it, whether it is building a model airplane, hiking through the woods, or catching a football. Often, though, that recreation becomes an obsession or even a compulsion. It may even become a career. Donald Douglas made a career out of building real airplanes. Ansel Adams and John Muir made careers out of hiking through the woods, photographing and writing about the wonders found there. Many have made careers out of playing, coaching, or popularizing football through the media.

The reasons that men have played football and the results gained from playing are often very different. For example, playing football is very different from building a house. When a person has the goal of building a house, he designs it and builds it. His goal is then completed. In football, a boy may begin to play because it is the most prestigious sport, or because his father wants him to play, or because it is the only thing to do after school. However, the outcome may be a feeling of accomplishment, the development of self worth, a college scholarship, or a lifetime job in playing or coaching.

Rick Mirer, the Seattle quarterback, when asked why he plays football and why it is important to him, replied, "I think most importantly because it's a challenge every single time you play and it's a great team sport. It's the best team sport there is. There is no satisfaction in winning alone that matches the feeling you get when you do it with ten other guys. It's definitely a challenge, and regardless of how many games you've won or lost, you still want to go out and play well every time you go out on the field."

Hall of Fame linebacker Sam Huff, of the Giants and Redskins, told us that he started playing just because it was expected. In the small West Virginia coal mining town where he grew up, boys were expected to go out for all three sports—football, basketball, and baseball. "I was pretty good at football and baseball, but I never could dribble, shoot, or jump! And I liked the contact inherent to football. I liked the contact in baseball, too. I was a catcher."

"I was always a competitor and always did everything I could to win. Football has never been a hobby with me. It has been a career. I played it in college because of my athletic scholarship and it was the only way I could go through school," Huff said.

Rick Mirer, Seattle Quarterback

The outcome of playing was different from why Sam originally was attracted to playing. He summarized his gratitude to the game by stating that "It taught me how to compete in life. It taught me patience. It taught me to give and take. But most of all, it taught me to survive in a tough world." Sam's drive for success has landed him the vice-presidency of Marriott Hotels.

Otto Graham, the all-time great Hall of Fame quarterback, started playing for the same reason as most boys – because it was fun. However, Otto had another motivation. His father had a great interest in music. Otto learned to play several instruments. While the violin and French horn did provide some enjoyment, they did not offer the excitement of sports which so many young men crave. So basketball and football soon took up more of his time than did the strings and woodwinds.

When Otto went to Northwestern on a basketball scholarship, he didn't decide to play football until he was a sophomore. Of course, he had great success as a quarterback. Paul Brown, when coaching Ohio State, was impressed, and when he became a pro coach, Otto was one of his recruits.

It was during World War II that Otto signed his first pro contract. He was a naval cadet who had been drafted by the Detroit Lions of the NFL. Paul Brown was a naval lieutenant coaching at Great Lakes Naval Training Station. As a cadet, Otto was making $75 a month. Paul offered him $1,000 to sign, $7,500 a year for two year and $250 per month until the war ended. It lasted only six more months.

Otto Graham

After his first pro year Coach Brown tore up his $7,500 contract and replaced it with a $12,000 agreement. When Otto finally resigned from playing he was making $25,000 a year, the highest salary in pro football. Even so, Otto was still playing for the fun of it.

Mel Hein, the All Pro Hall of Fame center of the New York Giants, attended Washington State College. In college, his coach got him a job which paid $25 a month, which was enough to pay half of his monthly tuition and expenses at the time.

Mel started his college career as the third string center on the freshman team. "I felt that I was as good as the other two centers, but evidently the coaches did not." During the last game of the year, against the University of Idaho, the varsity coach told the freshman coach to "put Hein in." So during the second half of the last freshman game, he finally got a chance. "I felt a surge of elation and strength when I entered the game. I wanted to prove to the head coach and to myself that I could play football. After the game Coach Hollingberry patted me on the shoulder and said, 'nice game'. This bolstered my ego and I determined to make good."

"During spring practice, I set a goal of being second string on the varsity in the fall. (The first string center was a three year starter.) During the summer, I got a job clearing trails for the forestry department. Each day I ran in the mountains. By the beginning of fall practice I was as tough and as hard as a rock. As a sophomore, I beat out the returning starter."

"My confidence, morale, and estimation of myself was now tops. My individual goal now was to become All-Coast and All-America. Our team also developed high goals. We won all of our games my senior year except the Rose Bowl where we lost to Alabama."

"I was tempted to play pro football because it paid more than teaching or coaching. I needed the money because I had accumulated a great deal of debt in working my way through college. I also wanted to marry my college sweetheart. This was the best move I ever made — we've been married for 54 years and are still going strong."

"I encountered the same problem in the pros that I faced in college. The Giants had two veteran centers and the squad limit of 25 allowed only two of us to make the team. I got a total of ten minutes of playing time in the two preseason games so I had to make it in the first league game or be cut. In that game, the starting center developed leg problems. The second string center made two bad passes to our tailback, so coach Steve Owens yelled at me 'Hein, do you think you can throw that damn ball back straight?' I didn't answer, just tore out on the field."

"All I could think of on offense was to snap the ball back straight then make a block. And on defense, I just tried to make the tackle. We won the game. And from then on, I played sixty minutes nearly every game. My personal goal was still to be the best that I could be."

Mel Hein

"Pride, hard work, and believing I could be the best helped me considerably during my career. But it is important that this desire should be kept to yourself. Action speaks louder than words. The man who 'mouths off' on what he can or will do is not respected by his fellow athletes."

Former Raider offensive line coach Sam Boghosian said that he played because he was always success-oriented. He was a hard working farm boy in Fresno. When he got the chance to play sports, he excelled. His chance for excelling was dealt a severe blow when he contracted polio at the age of eleven. Both he and his sister were taken to the hospital on the same day with polio. That same day his brother left that same hospital, dead from the infection of polio.

He was told that if he ever walked again it would be with a cane and that he would never be able to run. However, his drive to succeed helped Sam to overcome the paralysis in his lower leg. He excelled in baseball and was offered a pro contract but accepted a U.C.L.A. football scholarship and played guard on the 1954 national championship team, where he made All Coast and Academic All America. One of his fondest memories was playing in the East-West Shrine Game for the benefit of crippled children. "Participating in athletics has given me so much: an education, the joy of competition, and lifelong work as a football coach."

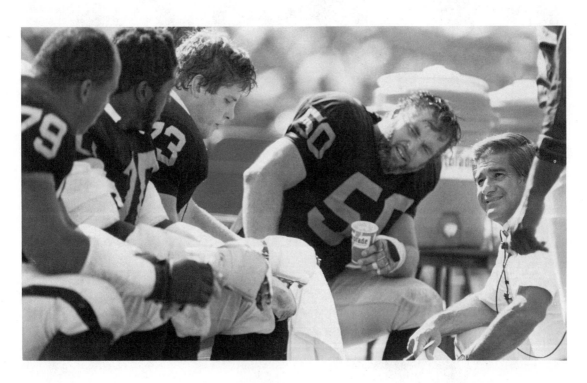

Sam Boghosian

Cortez Kennedy, Seattle's all-pro defensive lineman, said, "I play football because when I was growing up all my friends played the game. It was a big thing in Arkansas. As a kid, I always wanted to play and really began to love the game over the years. I play because I love the game, I can't let it go. There is no feeling like playing every snap with your teammates who care about you. I'm not here just to play, I'm here to be an impact player. I want to make a difference in our team. That's the way all of us Seahawks feel. We're all on the same path."

Former Raider defensive back coach and Hall of Famer Willie Brown said, "I played football for the love of the game, and for the excitement. And, of course, the college scholarship helped to get me closer to my goal of coaching. But on the way I learned so much while playing football: pride and confidence, the discipline to excel by working harder, patience and understanding, and the techniques of leadership. Football is certainly an enjoyable way to learn such essentials of living."

George Blanda, another football legend, played for the excitement of competition and for the camaraderie of his friends on the team. As with most people who have achieved in any area, George had a fire in him which lit the way for his teammates. Even during the grueling two-a-day practices when others were tired and listless, George was "up."

Cortez Kennedy   *Willie Brown*

Ken "Snake" Stabler was another one who enjoyed training camp. He was well-known for playing hard on the field, studying hard in the classroom, then playing hard when he wasn't on the field. He approached the game with a "let's kick hell out of them" attitude. His mood didn't change from Wednesday to Sunday or whether we were ahead or behind. "Snake" had nerves of steel and the heart of a lion and played the game to fulfil his natural talent.

Jim Plunkett made so many comebacks it was amazing. Not many athletes were counted out so many times and then came back to prove the "experts" wrong. He had a burning desire to be the best but to do it without fanfare. His pride and strong commitment brought him the Heisman Trophy then kept him in the Pro game for many years. He could have retired in 1978; however, he stuck it out and helped the Raiders win two Super Bowls. Jim played to meet and beat the challenges which the game presented.

Hall of Fame center Jim Otto, old "00", began to play for the recognition of being an athlete. As a young man from "the other side of the tracks," a person could gain recognition either from breaking the law or through athletics. "I chose football," he said.

Ken Stabler   *Jim Plunkett*

"I had a reputation, even in high school, of not backing down and of being able to play with pain. In my junior year in high school I played the whole season with a broken ankle. As a senior, I had head and neck injuries, but I wouldn't quit. During my second week in college I blew out my first knee. The next year the other one went, but I never quit."

"The combination of loving the game of football and desiring recognition kept me in the game through college and into the pros. Money was never really a factor. I just wanted to be best. First to get a scholarship to college, then to get a pro contract, then become All-Pro, then get into the pro Hall of Fame. I was lucky enough to achieve each goal."

"I still love the game, but I get my kicks now watching my son play, watching the Raiders, and remaining a part of the Raider family."

Jim Otto

Matt Millan has four Super Bowl rings: one with the 49ers, two with the Raiders, and one with the Redskins. He says that football helps you to learn a "zillion" things about yourself. One of the major things he has learned is to take care of the little things and the big things will take care of themselves.

He credits both his father and his high school coach, Andy Melosky, with developing his work ethic. His father would accept no marks in high school that were lower than 95 percent. His coach showed him the importance of working on the field.

Matt sets goals for himself daily. By working hard, he may be able to achieve them. As Matt himself said, it became clear to him at an early age that the expectations in life are greater than their realizations. "Nothing is as good as you expect." You must come to terms with that concept so that you don't give up when life isn't perfect. Just work harder at the game, at your studies, in your business, in your marriage. Move up, don't give up!

So there are many different reasons which these people have given for playing: fun, the enjoyment of the physical contact, the opportunity for hard fought competition, the recognition, the challenge of being the best, or a chance for a college scholarship.

The outcomes gained by the participants interviewed in this chapter include the development of self-esteem, the learning of patience, the encountering of the "give and take" of the game which taught them about the real world, the development of a sense of purpose in life and the place of discipline in accomplishing one's goals, the development of leadership abilities, and for some — a lifelong profession in the game.

In football, as in life, the participants must keep to the fundamentals. Even in the Super Bowl, if a player is not playing his best, he must go back to fundamentals. The same is true in life. Check your fundamentals. Are you doing what you should be doing?

It takes a special kind of person to enjoy the collisions which occur in football. The demands of the game require a different kind of courage than it takes to train for the Olympics in track or swimming. It takes a different kind of "guts" than are demanded when doing a double layout dismount from the high bar in a gymnastics competition.

It requires the "me against him" mind-frame of boxing or wrestling and adds to it the "us against them" feeling of a baseball team. The game provides the excitement of the "one for all and all for one" cry of the Three Musketeers and the feeling of brotherhood with one's teammates, while providing the satisfaction of having played one's best, win or lose, at the end of a game. Football sets forth the challenge of perfecting one's self and one's team.

Football requires long hours of preparation on the practice field and in the weight room, and teaches the maxim of success: we must have high aspirations, and we must work with a single-minded purpose toward our goals. The participants understand that maxim as they endure the thirst of a scorching August practice, as they wipe the blood from their faces in the heat of a fierce battle, and as they lose themselves in the team's collective emotions during their quest for victory: Nothing worthwhile ever comes easily. Later in life, as participants mature as citizens and fathers, they realize how important the game of football has been in making them who they are.

3

THE FASCINATION OF COACHING

Coaches are more than big kids who can't play anymore. They are people who share a passion for an enterprise. For professional coaches, that passion may be winning against many of the finest coaches in the game. For high school coaches, it may be the desire to work with the young men who come to them. The challenge of coaching may be in understanding the intricate complexities of the pro and college games, or in helping to mold young men into better citizens. There are many types of challenges and many sorts of satisfaction which spring from the game of football.

Only a few coaches make a great deal of money coaching. The great majority of coaches, from Pop Warner to the pros, do it for the love of the sport and the opportunity to work with boys and men who have a common purpose. Perhaps the best expression of this sentiment is a quote by John Robinson. Robinson left the head coaching position at U.S.C. for a three month stint as a university vice president, then returned to football as the head coach of the Rams. He said of the change, "The thing that shocked me the most was that outside of the sports world, there isn't the passion for what you do."

After taking a year out from football to sell real estate, Dan Reeves said, "I missed it. I don't think anything excites anybody as much as football does. Every week is a different situation, and if you play poorly you have a chance to redeem yourself the very next week."

One of the things that excites coaches is the challenge of molding a team from a group of individuals. Bill Walsh has a reputation for being an innovative strategist, and like many coaches, he has a penchant for drawing plays on tablecloths, napkins, and scraps of paper. He admits that, "Our fans like our technical football, but I'm really more concerned with two other things: the chemistry of the team and the proper evaluation and selection of talent. Nothing on this club is more important than the talent."

Coach Tom Flores of the Seattle Seahawks has enjoyed playing since he first touched a ball in the fifth grade. "I'm not sure if it was the game or the team camaraderie which is necessary for team competition which was most important to me. The fact that each player depended on the others was a big attraction for me. That same attraction carried into my professional playing and coaching careers. No sport has the team concept and team feeling that we have in football."

"Even when I was out of coaching, just being the general manager here in Seattle, what I missed most was the personal contact with the players and my fellow coaches. Game day would come, and I wasn't actively involved. I found that I really needed the excitement of preparation and of the game and I yearned for the personal contact. That's why I'm back on the field."

"Some people wonder why we coaches put in so much time. It's because we thrive on that feeling of purpose and the intensity of the drive of our players and the other coaches. When I was out of coaching for those few years I didn't miss playing with the 'X's and O's' so much. What I missed was the intimate contact with the committed people who play and coach the game."

"In the off-season, my normal workweek is only about 11 hours. I get to the office about seven in the morning and leave about six that afternoon. Of course, there are several weekends where I am committed for the whole time: when we go to the combine in Indianapolis each winter to test the potential draftees who are still in college, when we have mini-camps for our own players, and when there are the three weeks of NFL meetings. During the season, I still start my day about seven, but I stay longer at night. Monday and Thursday are early nights, I leave about seven. Tuesday and Wednesday, I stay until 10 or 11. Friday, we are usually travelling, so it makes another long day."

"Sunday, of course, is the day we look forward to. We are all peaked for a maximum effort. The home crowd cheers us on. What a great feeling! Even when we are away it is exciting. Sometimes you feel that the crowd respects or fears you. It gives you that extra bit of juice to give it everything you've got. The more I think of it the more I see that it is the people that excite me, whether it's my teammates or the fans. It is the intense involvement of people in this game that gives me my special enthusiasm for this great game of football."

Hank Stram, a winning Super Bowl coach with Kansas City and present day analyst for CBS football TV and radio programs, told us that what he liked best was the competitive aspect of the game, especially developing the strategies and finding the mismatches where his team could win the individual battles within the team game.

Hank said he always wanted to be associated with athletics. His father was a professional wrestler who wanted him to play baseball, not football. Although Hank played baseball throughout high school and for four years at Purdue, it was the special challenge of football that fascinated him.

One of the great influences on Hank was Tommy Harmon, the Heisman Trophy winner from Michigan and one of the great players of all time. Tommy was also from northern Indiana, and he was a lifeguard at the beach there during the summers. Hank would watch Tommy put on his heavy football shoes, walk to the softest sand he could find, and then run wind sprints in that soft sand until he was exhausted. Tony Zale, the great middleweight champion, was also from Gary. He was a good friend of Hank's father. Hank saw all of his fights. These two older mentors gave Hank models for success in athletics and in life and showed him the value of work and courage.

However, Hank almost got lost in the field of business. At the end of his senior year, he noticed an announcement in the job placement center stating that the Riddell Company was interested in a salesman who was an engineer. Hank applied and stated that he was a "physical engineer." He got the interview with Mr. Reifenach, the president of the company. Riddell was in the process of revolutionizing the helmet industry by replacing the old style leather helmets with the modern plastic head gear. They were also making the football shoes lighter by using split kangaroo leather rather than the full thickness cow hide shoes which were traditional. It was an exciting proposition.

Hank was offered the job. After accepting, the president asked him what a "physical engineer" was. So Hank, a physical education major at a recognized engineering university, told him that as a quarterback he engineered the physical bodies of his offensive team members. All got a good laugh. But as Hank left the office, Mr. Reifenach told him that he would make a good coach.

On returning to the Purdue campus, head coach Stu Holcomb called him into his office and offered him a one year coaching job for $3600. Hank grabbed it and canceled his job at Riddell. Mr. Reifenach accepted his resignation and wished him well but told him that the job was always his when he wanted it.

Hank was an assistant football coach and head baseball coach at Purdue for eight years. He left for the offensive coordinator's job at Southern Methodist University where he engineered a big upset over Notre Dame using his own modern theories of formations, the belly series, and a sophisticated passing attack. When the head coach left at the end of the year, the athletic director told Hank that he was his first choice for a head coach. However, Southern Methodist University was not yet ready for a Catholic head coach: the board of trustees wouldn't permit it.

Notre Dame called soon after, "I thought that they were interested in replacing their freshman coach so I was not interested, but it turned out that they were interested in an offensive coordinator, so I took the job. I always felt that you had to move upward and a freshman job would have been a downward move, but offensive coordinator at Notre Dame was an upward move." The head coach had been impressed with his offensive innovations. Hank, who had been offered a scholarship at Notre Dame as a player, had always felt close to the school so he took the job. After another coaching stint, he was interviewed by Lamar Hunt, the Texas billionaire, who was a primary figure in the origin of the American Football League which was to compete with the NFL. Hank was hired to coach Lamar's Dallas Texans which later became the Kansas City Chiefs.

"The fifteen years I spent with Lamar were great. I had total control — which is what you want as a head coach. Once you have control you can begin to work on the three things necessary to become a winner. First you must accumulate talent. You have to have the athletes. Second, you must properly evaluate the talent. A college quarterback may fit in better as a defensive corner or a wide receiver, or, as in the case of Paul Hornung, a running back. Then third, you must make the players the best they can be through the proper teaching of fundamentals."

"The joy of coaching, as I guess it is with most businesses, is in making the program a winner. Get the best athletes, teach them better than other coaches are teaching their players, and then once the season starts, checking the scouting reports and the game films and finding ways that your players can beat the other team's players one on one. And of course each week, after watching a hundred hours of the opponent's game films, find out what their team does in every tactical situation. It is the coach's job to analyze and digest what the team is doing differently than what they did last season. We spend the whole off-season analyzing the thinking of the opposing coaches and the techniques of opposing players. It is a great satisfaction to know that you have out-taught and out-thought the opposing coach, and that your team has functioned more efficiently than the opponents."

Another area of excitement and satisfaction for a coach, which is more evident at the high school and college levels, is the chance to make a positive change in the lives of the young men who play for the coach. John Pont, after 22 years as a college coach at Indiana, Northwestern, Miami of Ohio, and Yale and a few years of business, went back coaching in a high school. He loved it, because "I like making an impact on another person's life." Now John has accepted a new challenge in coaching. He has gone to Japan, where they have 600 teams playing American football.

Bob O'Connor, a coach with 40 years of coaching experience at every level, has coached with two Super Bowl coaches and with a national championship college team. He has found that the most satisfying level of coaching for him personally is at the high school level. As does his coauthor Flores, O'Connor believes it is the people that make the game what it is. "The boys and men who play football are several cuts above most young people because they have a purpose and they work hard to achieve that purpose."

Having coached club teams in Europe, O'Connor has found that the intensity of purpose was not as great for the European players as it is for the Americans. "In Europe football is a recreation; in America it is a passion. In Europe the players in the football club run the show; in America the coach, as teacher, is in control. I sincerely believe that the experienced educator in high school or college can make a real difference in the lives of his players."

Now coaching at Hollywood High School in California, O'Connor is seeing a different type of player. None of their fathers played football, so they don't have the parental pressure to play. They are pressured to go to work, or quit school and go to work. "But when I get a boy interested in college or get a gang member to choose football and education over fighting and drugs, it is very satisfying. Like Tom said, it's the people with whom you are involved that makes this such a great game. Most of us coaches feel the same — there is no team game like football and there is no game that can bring out the best in young men better than can football."

For many dedicated American men, the call to coaching is generated by the desire to make young people the best they can be, as football players, students, family members, and citizens. Young people must have ethical goals and the courage to achieve those goals. Just as with any other subject in the school curriculum, the class is no better than the teacher, and you can't be a better teacher or coach than you are a person.

Another area of great excitement to coaches is the planning of strategy to defeat an opponent. Walter "Piggy" Barnes, one of the linemen on "Greasy" Neale's revolutionary Eagle defense, tells about the strategy used to defeat the L.A. Rams in the 1949 championship game. The Rams had two of the finest quarterbacks who had ever played the game: Bob Waterfield and Norm Van Brocklin. "Greasy" feared the long ball of Van Brocklin to Elroy Hirsch or Tom Fears more than the shorter passes of Bob Waterfield. So his strategy was to cover the receivers closely and rush Waterfield hard, but not to hurt him. They wanted him in the game. So after every gentle sack, the Eagle rushers would help Bob to his feet. The Rams were unable to score and were defeated 14 to 0. And "Greasy" had outsmarted the legendary coach, Clark Shaughnessy. You might say that it "made his day."

Coaches, however, aren't the only ones to use pregame strategy. "Piggy" tells us that in the preparation for the next year's exhibition game rematch, the Rams worked out twice a day, but the Eagles only worked out once a day. It seems that "Greasy" loved to play golf and that quarterback Tommy Thompson was a "scratch" golfer. Team members chipped in a fair amount of money to bribe Tommy to challenge the coach to a golf game, then lose it. Each day the two played. Each day "Greasy" won. Each day the Eagles practiced once.

There is certainly a feeling of power which a coach derives when he develops a new concept of offense or defense. There is a feeling of satisfaction when he makes personnel evaluations which turn out to help the team. There is the joy felt when he can help a player or his family. Finally, there is the feeling of accomplishment when his team has won a game, especially a big game.

Robert Blackmon

4

THEORIES OF WINNING

All people have theories of winning in each area of their lives: a theory about how to get their two year old to stop spilling the milk, a theory about how to get his new neighbor to have dinner with him, or a theory about which horse to bet in the Kentucky Derby. Human relations, both on an individual and on a collective basis, often involve getting what we want or, in other words, winning.

Football coaches must have an overall theory on how they expect to win. As practice time is limited, coaches must determine their general approach to the game in advance so that the alignments, plays, and skills required can be designed and practiced.

Some coaches emphasize their defensive talents, some count on their knowledge of the kicking game, and many depend upon their offensive ideas to produce their victories. Some coaches believe that the best defense is a good offense. Others maintain that the best offense is a good defense. Advocates of both schools of thought have won national and professional championships.

FIELD POSITION THEORY

We often hear announcers talk about "good field position." This, of course, means that the ball is closer to the goal than it once was. This is, however, not what coaches mean by the "field position" theory of winning.

The field position theory of winning is probably as old as the game. Most of the legendary coaches of college football, including Knute Rockne, General Bob Neyland, Darrell Royal and Red Saunders, have been field position advocates.

Those who emphasize field position football generally want to keep their opponents bottled up in their own territory. It is these coaches' belief that it is extremely difficult to march a team 70 or 80 yards for a touchdown. The odds are that somewhere during that march there will be a penalty, a fumble, an incomplete pass, or an interception which will stall the drive. Field position advocates depend on the old adage that "to err is human" and hope that their opponent is particularly "human" on game day.

By emphasizing defense and kicking, the coaches hope to be able to slow down their opponents and force a miscue which will result in a stalled drive or a turnover. These coaches will generally position their best players on the defensive team, and they will spend a great deal of time perfecting the kicking game, especially punting.

There are many coaches who believe that it isn't that one team "wins" the game as much as the other team "loses" it. This is particularly true in close games. So the field position advocates try to "not lose" the game. For example, if the ball is inside their own 10 yard line, they may very likely punt it on the first down. Inside their 20, they will probably punt on second down, and inside their 35, they will punt on third down. Of course, because they spend so much time on the kicking game, they may well surprise their opponents by a fake punt on first, second or third down. If the opponent sends back one or two safetymen to field the punt, their defense is weakened against the run and the pass at the line of scrimmage, so an occasional fake might get good yardage.

The quick kick is another important element in the field position general's arsenal. As the idea is to keep the opponent deep in his own territory and because a well executed quick kick can gain 60 yards or more (compared to the 35 yards expected on a punt), the often orphaned quick kick is a favored son to a field position coach.

The field position coach will generally divide the field into certain zones. As has been noted, inside their 35 yard line is going to be an early kicking down. Between the 35 and the 50 is an area where "safe" plays are called. Once past midfield, a team will probably open up and may throw some passes. Inside the opponent's 35 yard line, they will generally assume that they are in "4 down territory," meaning that less than three yards have to be made per play in order to get a first down. The team may then revert to a more conservative running game.

Knute Rockne divided the field into five 20-yard areas. From his own goal to the 20, he would kick on first down. From his 20 to his 40, he wouldn't pass and would punt on second or third down. When the ball was in the 40s, he might pass and would only punt on fourth down. From the offensive 40 to the 20, he would use some trick plays or go for a field goal if his offense was stopped. From the opponent's 20 to the goal, he would use the plays most likely to score.

Darrell Royal, a former Texas coach, thought of the field in three zones. From his goal to the 35, he wanted to get the ball across the 50 in any way possible: safe runs, passes and, if necessary, the punt. Between the two 35 yard lines, which he called "the alumni zone," he considered it the duty of the coach to entertain the fans. From the offensive 35 to the goal, it was four down territory and they had to score.

"Play it safe and avoid mistakes" is the maxim which guides the thinking of the field position coach. The objective of his offensive ideas is to slow the opponent. His offensive ideas tend to be conservative. He is likely to use an offensive attack based on power, with an emphasis on double team blocking (putting two of his players against one member of the opposition). He is football's answer to Aesop's tortoise, who as you may remember beat the hare in their classic contest.

Players are told, "Don't lose the game." Such thinking is often more effective than the average person realizes. A few years ago Lawrence High School of Lawrence, Kansas won more than 50 straight games based on the philosophy of "playing for the tie." Their objective was to let the other team lose the game. Coach Al Woodard emphasized that "we won't lose it." As the game of football generally involves over 130 plays with 22 players in on each play, there are ample opportunities for errors. The old coaching adage that "football is a game of inches" indicates the small margin of error which can be the difference between winning and losing.

BALL CONTROL THEORY

Coaches who center their philosophy on ball control are more interested in a safe offense. They hope to make 3 1/2 yards on each of three running downs or five yards on two of their three passing downs so that they can get the first down. Naturally, they want to avoid mistakes such as penalties (which would force them out of their short yardage theory) or turnovers (which would take away the ball).

Their emphasis is on safe running and safe passing plays. The University of Oklahoma teams of the 50s, under Bud Wilkinson, were masters of the ball control running attack. Most college and professional teams today are ball control teams. The more conservative offenses of the Rams, the Bears, and the Cowboys are illustrations of such running attacks, as the BYU teams of LaVell Edwards or the San Francisco teams of Bill Walsh are examples of good ball control passing attacks.

On paper, every offensive play can easily gain four yards. On the blackboard, every lineman makes his block and the ball carrier never fumbles. The problem is that players seldom perform as well as the O's on the chalkboard. On the chalkboard the O's always beat the X's, at least when the offensive coordinator has the chalk.

THE BIG PLAY APPROACH

While all coaches have their stock of safe runs and passes, some coaches believe that the higher percentage chance of winning lies in striking for the touchdown on one play. The Raiders are such a team. Whether it is the long bomb, the deep reverse, the trick play, or the 20 yard pass which "might break," getting an immediate touchdown is always on the mind of the "big play" oriented coach.

While some coaches contemplate the "big play" with more prayer than preparation, the true big play advocates have planned for the event. Each long scoring play has been practiced and evaluated hundreds of times before it is used in a game.

The advantages of big play thinking go beyond the chance of the quick score. The defensive coordinators and their teams know that the big play team may go for it all on any play. Therefore, they must always defend against that long quick score, which means that they often are not ready for the basic ball control game. Their defensive backs may not support on the run quite as quickly because of their fear of the "bomb." Their defensive linemen or backers may not pursue quite as recklessly because of their fear of the reverse. If they rush the passer over-aggressively, they may open up the draw or the screen pass. So, the threat of the big play makes the ball control game more effective.

When you are watching the game, it may appear that the big play teams are going for the "bomb" half of the time. It's true that they do send receivers deep often, but generally they expect to throw deep only five or six times a game.

COMBINATIONS OF THEORIES

Most coaches will adopt more than one approach during the season. Perhaps the opponent is very strong, so a "big play" approach is viewed as the only way to win. The coach may use a fake punt or put in trick plays on the assumption that it is his only hope.

Even the most diehard field position coaches will go for the big play sometimes. It helps to keep the defense honest. Also, the big play advocates will use lots of ball control plays. But the day that the big play coach punts on a first down will be the day when our million dollar quarterbacks refuse pay raises.

Successful coaches look at the probabilities of success for a certain type of play. For example, a field position coach might throw long from his own end zone about once in every ten years. He knows that the opposing coach is aware of his conservative bent, so once in a while he may throw long.

WINNING WITH THE RUN OR THE PASS

Both running attacks and passing attacks can be conservative or daring. Dive or power plays are "safe," especially if the runner carries the ball with both hands so he won't fumble. Safe passing attacks opt for lots of short passes to the backs away from the major pass defenders. On the other hand, option football (such as the veer and wishbone) increases the teams' chances of fumbles but increases the chances for long gainers. Big play passing teams don't worry about the interception as much, because when a long pass is intercepted it is about the same as having punted the ball. Of course big play coaches prefer the long completion to the long interception, when given the choice.

Running advocates say that there are three things that can happen when you pass, and two of them (the incomplete pass or the interception) are bad. To avoid the incomplete pass or the interception, these coaches stick to the run. Passing enthusiasts, on the other hand, believe that a good passing attack can more easily be put together with lesser players than can a good running attack. Consequently many coaches pass because of weakness, rather than strength.

Another consideration for coaches is the weather. No matter where your team plays, you must plan for days that are cold or rainy, especially if your team focuses on a passing attack. If you are guaranteed of playing every game on clear and windless 70 degree days, your chances of opting for a passing attack are greatly increased.

As there are so many teams passing, many people believe that passing is the best way to win. While most coaches express their hope for a balanced attack (gaining nearly equal amounts of yardage from the run and the pass), in practice the running game has a lot going for it. In college football, the ten top running teams in the country generally win an average of 80 percent of their games, while the ten top passing teams generally win an average of 50 percent. At the pro level, it has been found that teams that run forty times in a game will win 90 percent of the time. How many times do the the Cowboys lose when Emmit Smith gains over 100 yards?

A coach at the youth or the high school level will have to do some hard thinking before deciding on the general theory of his approach to winning. He must consider the type of players he will work with (their toughness and their skills), the weather, and his own competencies and beliefs. At the college level, the coach can recruit for many of his needs so he may not be as influenced by player inadequacies. At the professional level, the coach is nearly precluded from choosing a pure field position approach because the fans come to see the team score, not to see them punt on first down.

The coach's decision on how his team can best win is essential in determining his theories of offense, defense, and kicking, and it will play an essential part in the development of his week-to-week strategy for upcoming opponents. When a coach decides to punt on fourth-and-one on his opponent's 45, that decision was probably made months, or even years before, as part of his overall theory of winning, and the boos from the fans are not likely to persuade him to do otherwise.

Joe Nash

5

THEORIES OF OFFENSIVE FORMATIONS

FORMATIONS, SHIFTING AND MOTION

One of the weapons in the coach's arsenal for winning is choosing formations that will allow his players to get a mismatch against an opponent. One formation may allow for better blocking angles against one team's defense. Another formation or a type of man in motion may allow a coach to put a faster receiver against a slower linebacker.

Perhaps the defensive coach rotates his players to the wide side of the field in certain situations. The offensive coach may then set a formation which is likely to result in that type of rotation, but call a play which attacks the weakness of the secondary.

Perhaps a coach can shift his offensive backfield one direction but the defense does not adjust to the new strength of the offense. A play to the shifted side may then work. Or, if the defense over-adjusts to the shift or the motion, plays can be called back to the other side.

Getting a mismatch by a formation or by getting a strong player against a weaker one is a major objective for most coaches in their game planning. Obviously a coach chooses a formation which will best allow him to attack most effectively according to his theory of attack.

Today's pro teams nearly always use a formation which will allow three immediate pass receivers into the defensive secondary. And often they set up to allow four or even five men to attack the pass defense of the opponents. College or high school wishbone offenses may keep both ends tight and all three backs in the backfield in order to make their running games more effective.

We are all familiar with the variations of the T-formation which we see in most football games. But let's go back a few years and look at some of the formations which have been used—some of which are still being used by some high school and college coaches. Most of these were in use in the 1920s and 30s, but note how modern formations have used ideas from fifty years ago.

Rockne's Notre Dame box

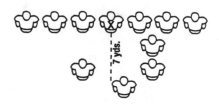

Harvard's short punt

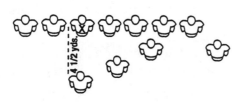

Pop Warner's single wing

Warner's double wing

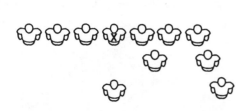

One of Rockne's passing formations

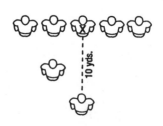

Minnesota's spread

Louisiana State's formation

Yale's formation

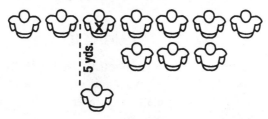

Penn State's six formation

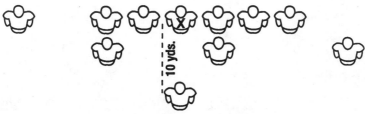

Idaho's formation

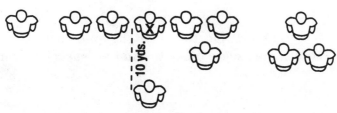

Princeton's formation

There were more variations of formation in the past than there are now! Does that mean that we are all copycats now—or have we reached the "ultimate" in offensive alignment? Probably neither, because the offense must align itself to attack the defense. As the defense adjusts to strength, so must the offense change its strength.

When the "nickel" defense (using five rather than four defensive backs) came into play to stop the pass on an obvious passing down, many offensive teams adjusted by using a running formation and a running play. And when the defense substitutes an additional lineman to stop the run in a short yardage situation, many teams will exploit the pass.

SELECTING THE OFFENSIVE FORMATION

Before starting an offensive play, the coach must decide which offensive formation to use. He may choose a formation because it is especially advantageous for that play, or he may choose a formation just to see how the defense adjusts so that any weakness can be exploited on an ensuing play.

For example, on an off-tackle power play there is an advantage to having a tight wingback next to the end in order to double team the defender. If this is done, does the defense bunch up to stop the obvious power of the formation? If so, it may be opening itself to a pass from that formation.

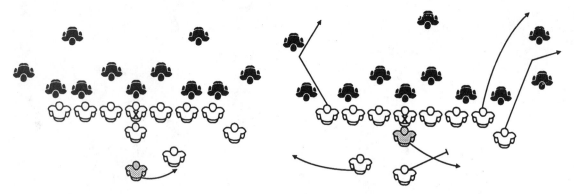

Wingback set versus Okie 5-2 – no defensive adjustment so it is open to the run

Wingback set versus Okie — defense adjusts by rotating its backfield, exposing it to a quick pass

The tight formation (T, wing T, single wing) has the advantages of running power, good faking, and quick counters, but they lack the quick pass threat. Teams with good passers and receivers are more likely to want at least three immediate receivers threatening the defense.

Since it is more difficult for a back than it is for a lineman to block a defensive lineman, most coaches prefer to have at least six linemen near the ball. So they will split one end and flank a back. Other coaches want to keep three backs close to the quarterback so they split both ends and set one back as a wingback. They lose a little on the blocking, but gain on the faking and countering aspects of their attacks.

Pro set (tight end, split end and flanker)

Two split ends and a wingback

Coaches will set flankers not only to open up the pass, but also to spread the defense. If you can get the opponents to put a cornerback and a linebacker far to one side of the field to stop your pass threat, it is going to be difficult for them to stop a run up the middle or to the opposite side of the field.

More and more we are seeing four immediate receivers. When a coach wants four immediate receivers he has the choice of putting two on each side of the center or of "going trips"—with a core of triple receivers on one side.

Following are some examples of balanced four receiver sets:

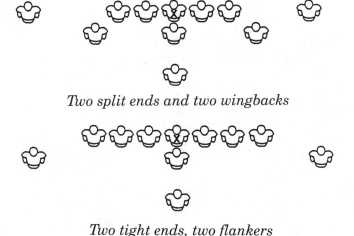

Two split ends and two wingbacks

Two tight ends, two flankers

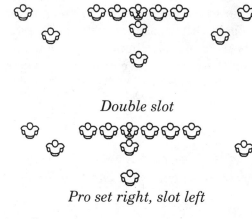

Double slot

Pro set right, slot left

Examples of "trip sets":

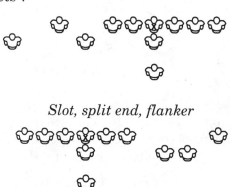

Slot, split end, flanker

Two slots and a split end

And, of course, you can use five immediate receivers—putting the quarterback under the center or in a shot gun set.

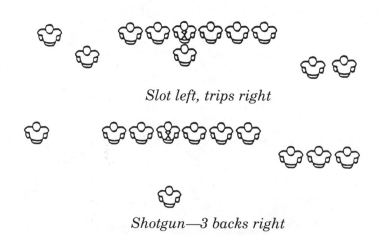

Slot left, trips right

Shotgun—3 backs right

PLACEMENT OF THE LINEMEN

The rules say that the offensive team must have at least seven men on the line of scrimmage and that the end men on the line are eligible for passes. Today most teams use balanced lines, with a guard, tackle and end on each side of the center. When a team occasionally goes unbalanced, it often catches the defense off guard.

Balanced line

Unbalanced line right

Shift to eight man line (wingback moves up to make him a more effective blocker)

Unbalanced line with guards and tackles over

Shift to unbalanced from pro set

Unbalanced with snapper as the end

The spacing of the linemen is another factor for a coach to consider. If the linemen are close to each other, they can double team block and cross block more effectively. If they are split wider, they spread the defense better and create either holes or blocking angles. If the defensive lineman splits with the offensive man, a hole is created. If he splits only part way, perhaps playing on the inside shoulder of the offensive man, a blocking angle is created. Most offensive linemen are taught to be creative in their splits—often splitting wider on the side away from the play, to put the defender further from the hole.

Tight line

Split line

Creating a hole with line splits   *Creating blocking angles*

Another factor in determining the placement of the linemen is their strengths and abilities of the linemen. In a basic T formation the linemen generally have the same assignments on either side of the center. But in some attacks, such as the single wing, power I, and some pro attacks the assignments may be quite varied from one side to the other.

On one team the strong side of the line may emphasize double team blocks while the "weak" or "quick" side of the line specializes in pulling, one-on-one blocks, cross blocking, downfield blocking, or other such skills. When the two sides of the line have different types of blocking responsibilities they will "flip flop."

A flip flopping team will always have their "strong side" linemen on the side of their basic power plays and their "quick side" linemen on the side to which they will counter or run quick plays. Teams which flop their line will do so by crossing their linemen as they break the huddle or by serpentining them. (The strong end or wing back leads the team in a motion which looks like a serpents motion.)

Straight huddle break — strong right   *Crossing break — strong left*

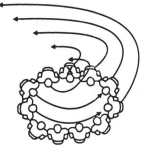

Serpentine break — strong left

SETTING THE BACKS IN A FORMATION

If all three backs are set in the normal T formation there will be a great threat to the defense in quickness and countering. Each back removed from the three back formation reduces the running attack, while adding to the passing threat. When a coach decides to remove a fullback, he gives up the buck, the fullback trap, the counter and slant. When he removes a halfback, he gives up the dive threat and the quick pitch to that side, and the halfback traps and counters to the other side. The defense knows this and can afford to reduce its defense in the areas where it is not threatened.

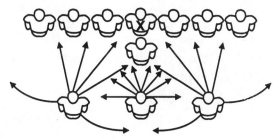

Here are the possible paths of backs in a "full house" T. Removing one of them eliminates several possible plays.

Once the coach decides where he wants to set the backs, he may have to adjust their position somewhat by what he wants the back to do. For example, a very fast back in a dive play might beat the quarterback to the hole, so he might have to be set a foot or two deeper than normal. In most offensive running attacks the timing of the backs is very important so backfield coaches will often use "cheats" to make the timing better.

Examples of "cheating" the backs are: setting a halfback wider or deeper when the quick pitch is used to his side; moving a halfback up or in for certain trap plays or for pass blocking; or moving the fullback up when he is faking and blocking.

Halfback cheat out   *Fullback cheat up*

As a spectator, you can often pick up the cheats and get a good idea of what the offensive play will be. The offense hopes that defenders won't see their alignment changes.

Setting the feet of the backs and the placement of the hands is also a factor in their effectiveness. In a two point stance, the back will not have his hand on the ground. This allows him to see the defense better and to get wide fast, but he can't go forward as fast—so he may have to line up closer to the line of scrimmage. One of the problems with the two point stance is that the back often becomes eager and is in motion early, causing an unnecessary penalty.

If the back is expected to go forward, right or left, his feet should be parallel to the line of scrimmage. If he is expected to go only forward or to his right he can have his right foot back. (It is slower to go to his left from this stance.) If he is going to go laterally much of the time he would not want much weight on his hands. But if he is going forward he might well get into a sprinter's stance.

Defenders, of course, look for keys from the backs. Does he have extra weight forward (indicating he will dive), is he cheated wide (for a possible pitch), is he tipping off where he is going by his eyes or by his body lean? Coaches, in scouting or in evaluating films, look for such tips.

When a coach is running an I pro attack he may put his tailback from 4 1/2 to as far as seven yards back. If he wants the back to hit a certain hole, the coach will have him closer. But if he wants him to pick his hole, depending on how the defense adjusts to the play, he will be deeper. The U.S.C. attack under John McKay and John Robinson uses this deep set which allows the skilled back to improvise. It takes a very intelligent coach to let Mike Garrett or Marcus Allen run where he sees an opening.

SHIFTING THE OFFENSE

Knute Rockne is given credit for developing the backfield shift. After lining up in a T formation the backs would shift right or left into their Notre Dame box. The ball would be snapped as they were finishing the shift. This put a great strain on the defense to adjust to the power in time for the play. (The rule now is that after a shift a player has to remain motionless for a full second—so that the defense can adjust to the new formation.)

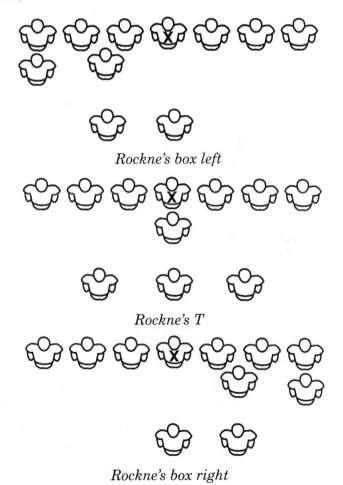

Rockne's box left

Rockne's T

Rockne's box right

At Illinois, Bob Zuppke used a line shift to help spring Red Grange, to his legendary running exploits. The guards were set behind the line then they shifted into the right or left gap to give an unbalanced line for the "galloping ghost" to run behind.

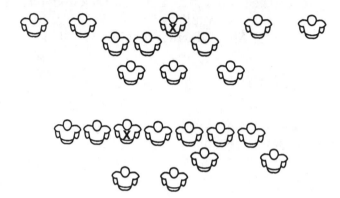

Examples of the Illinois shift to an unbalanced line slot set or to an eight man line.

Howard Jones, of Iowa, also had some interesting ideas on shifting his offensive people. This was the same Howard Jones who was hired by the University of Southern California and began their rise to football fame. At U.S.C., Coach Jones worked with such immortals as Cotton Warburton and John Wayne.

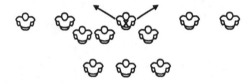

The Iowa pre-shift position

To unbalanced line single wing

To a 9 man unbalanced line   *To unbalanced line—backs opposite*

Today many teams will use backfield shifts to upset the defensive strategy.

Wing T left   *Shifting to wing T right*

Perhaps no modern team has exploited the shift as much as the Dallas Cowboys under Tom Landry. They would line up in one set, then everybody would move. The linemen would adjust their splits, the backs would move to another position. They knew where they are going, but none of the rest of the coaches did. They might shift to an I, split backs, pro set, one back or any other set they could devise.

As defenses became more specialized with a strong safety, strong cornerback, strong and weak linebackers, and perhaps strong and weak defensive linemen—all with special responsibilities, it was inevitable that someone would shift to upset such defenses. Since the defenders declare the offense "strong" to the side of the tight end, many teams would declare the tight end to one side, let the defense set, then move the tight end to the other end of the line. This movement of one man could force the defense to move at least two defenders—and probably six or more men.

Pre-shift with tight end right

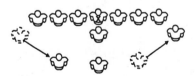

Shift to tight left

This shift might force the movement of the strong and free safeties, the strong and weak side inside and outside backers, a "rover back" (if one is used), and perhaps the cornerbacks.

THE USE OF MOTION

American football teams are allowed to have a back in motion going parallel to the line of scrimmage or moving backward. (Canadian rules permit more than one player to go in motion at the same time—a factor which is directly responsible for the high insanity rate among Canadian defensive coordinators.)

Motion can be used to change formation by changing the strength of the formation (changing from a flanker to a slot or a slot to a flanker formation).

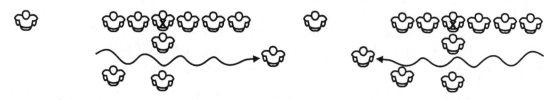

Flanker set motioned to slot set   *Slot set to flanker*

Motion can be used to stretch the formation from tight to a wide set, or to reduce the formation from a flanker set to a tight set.

Stretching the formation from a wing to a flanker   *Reducing the formation from a flanker to a wing*

When teams don't adjust to the motion, they make themselves vulnerable to the offense changing the formation strength then attacking to strength. It is amazing how often teams will disregard the change in formation strength.

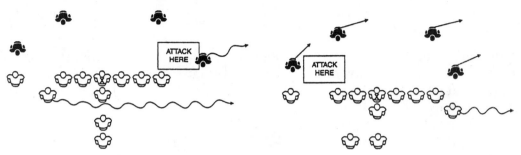

A balanced defense which doesn't adjust to a change in formation strength. (Attack towards the motion.)

A defense adjusting to motion, which doesn't change the strength of the formation. (Attack away from the motion.)

Sometimes "short motion" is used. This is almost like a shift. Here is an example of the types of motion which a wingback could use: (1) short motion to the halfback position, (2) short motion to a power I formation, (3) motion to the slot area, (4) motion to the flanker area.

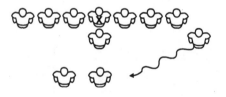

(1) motion to halfback spot

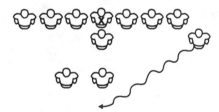

(2) motion to tailback spot

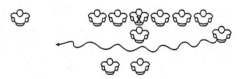

(3) motion to slot area

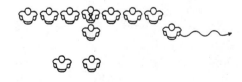

(4) motion to flanker area

While a back in short motion cannot run a dive play, he can run a trap or counter to the other side and can certainly run a sweep. This type of motion is used extensively by wing T teams.

Motion can also be used to bring a slot back or flanker into a position where he can execute an outside in trap block. This is a great surprise to the lineman being trapped, and often a greater surprise to the flanker who learns that he can block as well as catch passes.

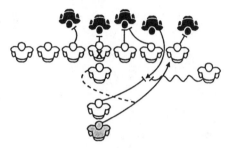

Outside in motion, with trap block

Another major use of motion is to determine whether the defense is playing a man to man or a zone defense on that play. This makes it easier for the quarterback and the receivers to determine which patterns will work best on that play. If a zone shows perhaps a deep curl will be run. If man-to-man shows, perhaps a crossing pattern or a comeback would work best.

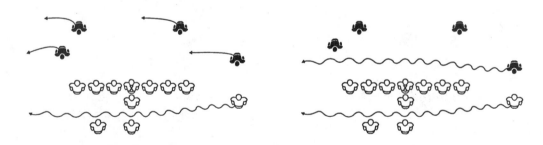

Crossing motion—defense indicates it is in a zone defense   *Crossing motion—defense shows it is in man coverage*

Modern day teams are usually multiple formation teams which use a good deal of motion. A good part of the chess match element of the game is involved in setting one's formations and evaluating the opponent's adjustments to them. Finding and exploiting the weaknesses in a defensive team's adjustments to formations can often be the key to winning the offensive battle.

6
THEORIES OF DEVELOPING
A RUNNING ATTACK

In spite of the prevalence of the pass in pro and college programs, most teams still win with running. A good running attack forces the defense to stop it first before thinking about the pass. It keeps the linebackers on the field rather than letting five or six defensive backs into the game to stop the pass. When a team makes 200 yards on the ground—it almost never loses.

Theories on running attacks can be categorized as either power, quickness or finesse. All coaches will use at least two of these theories, but in most offenses one is emphasized.

The power game is predicated on the idea of having more men than your opponent at the point of attack. Most power teams use double team blocks by the linemen and/or blocking backs to accomplish this.

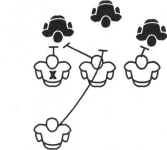

A double team block

A double team with an isolated line-backer blocked by a fullback

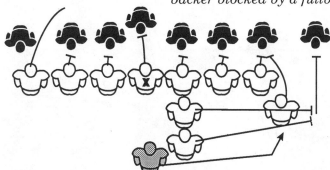

A Tennessee single wing power play with two double blocks

Quickness advocates emphasize getting the ball carrier to the line of scrimmage before the defense has a chance to react and pursue. The Split T dive play, the fullback buck, and the quarterback sneak are examples of quickness plays.

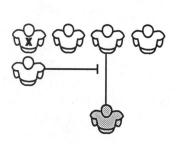

Split-T dive

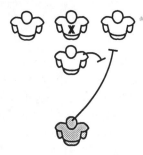

Fullback buck

Quarterback sneak

The finesse game utilizes trickery or "reads" to fool the defense. Traps, counters, and reverses, as well as option series fall into this category.

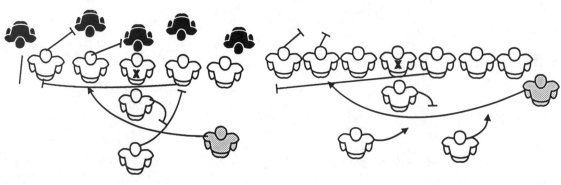

Halfback trap   *Wingback reverse*

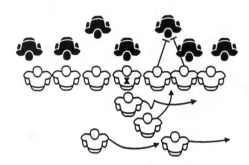

Wishbone triple option

Now for a bit more detail on these three approaches to the running attack.

THE POWER GAME

Probably the most potent power game within the college ranks was the Tennessee single wing offense. The basic series was an off-tackle play in which the strong end and wingback double teamed the defensive tackle. The blocking back and fullback tandem blocked the defensive end (who was set up by the tailback faking to go wide, then cutting back behind the tandem block). Both guards would pull through the hole to block for the tailback.

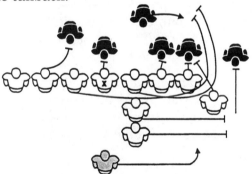

Single wing off tackle power play

The term "off tackle" means outside the defensive tackle. Years ago, plays were named by the defensive position that was meant to be attacked, and the defensive tackles always played in the area of the offensive ends. Today, plays are nearly always called for the point where the offensive lineman is positioned because there are so many different types of defenses. Therefore, the off-tackle play usually involves the end blocking with his tackle or a wingback. The man they block may be a defensive end, a linebacker, or the defensive tackle. So today "off tackle" seldom means "off" the defensive tackle. Coaches just refused to change their old terminology as the defensive alignments and offensive numbering systems changed. It's similar to people calling all refrigerators "Frigidaires" or ice boxes.

The favorite inside power play was the fullback buck with a wedge block. On this play, the linemen formed a shoulder-to-shoulder wedge and pushed aside anyone in their path.

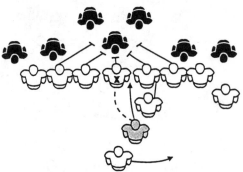

Wedge on the offensive center

Despite all of its power, the Tennessee wing hit the hole slowly. This forced the center to snap the ball backward before blocking, which was much tougher than being a T-formation center. For the Tennessee wing to be really effective, the team also had to have a durable and outstanding triple threat back at tailback. The 1950 U.C.L.A. team lost its four top tailbacks for the season before their first game. By the end of the season its starting tailback was the former eighth string tailback. But the former eighth string tailback, sophomore Ted Narleski, made the All Coast team. For those who could survive the punishment, playing single wing tailback was the ultimate football position. The single wing tailback was the equivalent of a combination pro quarterback and an I formation tailback.

The Coach Tom Nugent's Maryland I formation was also a powerful attack. In the Maryland offense, there were four backs lined up behind the center. Don Coryell, when coaching Whittier College, used a similar attack. A few years ago when he was coaching the San Diego Chargers, he brought some of these plays back.

Here is a sample of the power which could be generated by such an attack. Note the similarities with the single wing power.

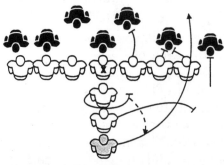

Off tackle play

While at U.S.C., John McKay combined the I formation with the pro style passing game (Pro I). This gained him a passing advantage but lost some of the running attack power. Here are two samples of power plays from the U.S.C. I formation: the off tackle play and an inside isolation play where the linebacker is not blocked by the linemen but is isolated, then blocked by the fullback—with the tailback having the option of running to either side of the fullback's block.

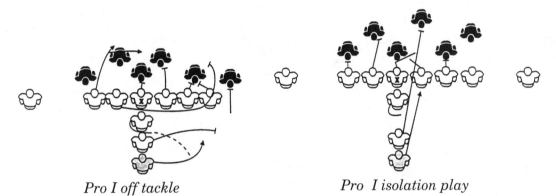

Pro I off tackle   *Pro I isolation play*

The disadvantages of the I formation are that it can't get to the outside quickly and it doesn't have the capability of crossing the backs in faking actions — so it is easier for the linebackers to key.

The power I formation is seldom used as the primary attack, but it is often used by I pro offenses in short yardage situations. Here, the flanker is brought in to the halfback spot. From this position, the flanker and the fullback can lead the tailback to his side of the line, or the fullback and tailback can lead the halfback to the other side of the line.

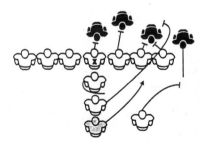 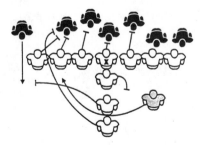

Power I—halfback lead   *Power I—tailback lead*

The off tackle power game from the T formation was probably best emphasized by Vince Lombardi's attack at Green Bay in the 1960s.

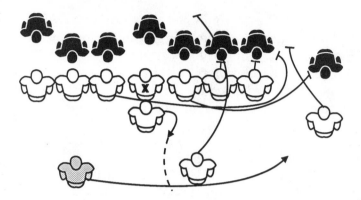

The Green Bay sweep, could be cut off tackle or continued as a wide sweep—depending on how the outside linebacker was blocked

It is easy to see how the teams that use the T formation have utilized the blocking patterns from the single wing power play. The disadvantage modern pro formations with several players set wide is that each time a back is flanked as a wide receiver a potential blocker is lost. Also, if the quarterback is not called upon to act as a blocker (because the coach is afraid that he will get hurt), another blocker is lost.

THE QUICKNESS GAME

The quickness game is indigenous to the T formation. Because the center hands the ball to the quarterback, he can also handoff to any of his other backs—without the backs waiting for the ball to get to them, as in the single wing.

With a quickness attack there will be no special power. Nearly always the blocks will be one-on-one, and those blocks don't have to be sustained because the back will be at the hole in half a second. If the play is designed to hit between the guards, the fullback will carry it. If is to go just inside or outside of the tackle, the halfback will carry it. This halfback dive was the basic play of the Split T attack as developed by Don Faurot at Missouri, then popularized at Oklahoma by the late Bud Wilkinson.

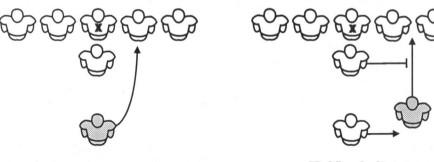

Fullback buck   *Halfback dive*

From the I formation it is the fullback who is the quick hitter. He can go to the same side as the tailback or to the opposite side—in a counter action.

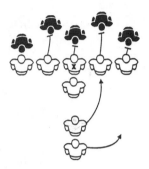

I fullback buck (or drive)

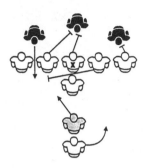

I fullback counter trap (a quick finesse type play)

Getting wide quickly is done with the quick pitch, a play designed by Hamp Pool, the former Los Angeles Rams coach. If the defensive end plays close to the offensive tackle, he can usually be flanked by the quick pitch. (Note: if there is a fullback, he will usually run towards the defensive end to threaten him, making it easier for the ball carrier to skirt around him.)

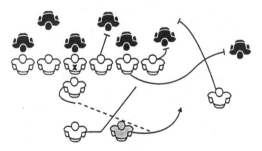

Quick pitch

THE FINESSE GAME

Every offense has some elements of the finesse game. There is always at least one play which finishes in the opposite way from which it starts. This makes the linebackers more cautious in their pursuit of the ball carrier. By keeping the opponent's defense aware of the countering action, they will be a bit less effective in stopping the offense's primary power or quickness plays.

If the offense uses a wingback, he will be the primary person used in the countering actions. When the wingback, end or wide receiver become the ball carrier, it is called a reverse. On the following pages are examples of reverse plays:

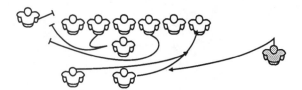

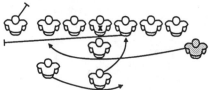

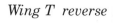

Reverse to wide receiver from a pro set T   *Wing T reverse*

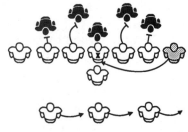

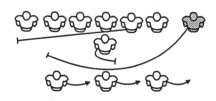

Inside reverse to a tight end   *End around*

Below are some examples of countering actions; actions using the set backs rather than the wingback, ends or wide receivers.

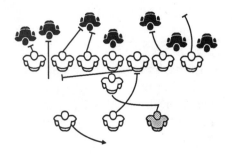

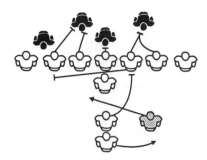

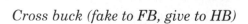

Cross buck (fake to FB, give to HB)

Cross buck from Power I

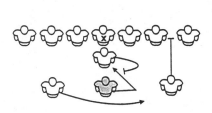 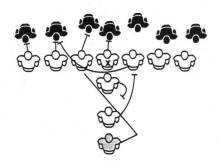

Fullback counter from Split T dive series   *Tailback counter from Pro I formation
(used if defense is keying the fullback)*

Another part of the finesse game involves what has come to be known as option football. In this type of offense, the quarterback must determine whether to give or keep the ball depending on the action of a defensive player. On wide plays from the Split T attack, the quarterback fakes to the diving halfback and fakes to the fullback (who is a running off tackle). When the quarterback comes to the defensive end, he has to decide whether to keep the ball and cut upfield or pitch the ball to the trailing halfback. The man who is being optioned (in this case, the defensive end) is not blocked.

The quarterback must determine whether the end will take him (if so, he will pitch) or take the trailing halfback (if so, he will keep it and run, perhaps pitching to the halfback further up the field). Coaches should give the quarterback a key to help his decision.

Coaches use different keys to help their quarterbacks make play decisions. For example, if the quarterback can see the front numbers of the defensive end (indicating that the end is facing the QB and is probably going to tackle him), he should pitch the ball. Or perhaps the key will be that if the end is closer than two yards from the tackle, he should pitch the ball. The key might be that if the end is on the line of scrimmage the quarterback should pitch the ball, but if the end penetrates into the backfield, he will keep it.

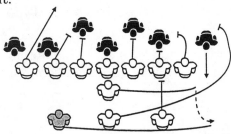

Split T option (defensive end close to QB). QB options to pitch.

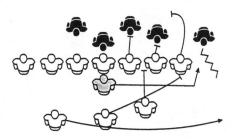

Split T option (end playing loose). QB options to keep the ball and run.

During these plays, the fullback can be used as a lead blocker for the halfback or he can run the slant at the defensive end, then block in on a linebacker or lead the halfback downfield.

The speed option does not rely on an inside dive fake. This play is generally run from a two back set. What the speed option loses in the inside fake, it gains with the addition of a blocker.

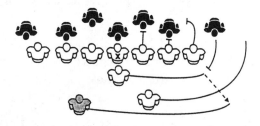

Speed option to halfback

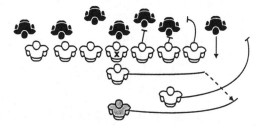

Speed option to fullback

Another option is the freeze option. In this option, a back runs inside to "freeze" the linebackers where they are so that they can be blocked by the offensive linemen. Then the quarterback runs at the defensive end and options him. This greatly cuts down on the pursuit of the defensive team. A number of I formation teams now use this type of play.

The ultimate play in option football is the triple option. The wishbone and the veer are the major triple option attacks, although some teams run a triple option from an I formation.

In a triple option, both the defensive end and the tackle are left unblocked. Because of this there are extra offensive linemen who can double team the opposing defenders, especially the linebackers. This gives this type of finesse attack some of the elements of a power attack.

The wishbone attack, named for the wishbone shape of the backfield, was designed at the University of Texas. It is often considered the ultimate running attack. Auburn used it with great success until Bo Jackson's senior year—when they went to the I-formation to use Bo's sensational skills.

Although the wishbone attack is very effective, the quarterback can take a beating because he is running a good deal of the time. Colleges can recruit a number of quarterbacks to play the position, but the pros don't have this luxury. A pro team generally can't afford to have more than three quarterbacks on the roster. And they are not about to take the chance of having a multimillion dollar player be tackled hundreds of times a year while running the option play.

In the wishbone, the quarterback reaches back to the fullback and puts the ball against the fullback's belly as the quarterback reads the defensive tackle. If the tackle has an outside responsibility, the ball is given to the fullback. If the tackle comes in to stop the fullback, the quarterback takes the ball back, while the fullback blocks the tackle. The quarterback then moves quickly down the line to option the defensive end. At that point, he reads the defensive end, just as he did in the Split-T option.

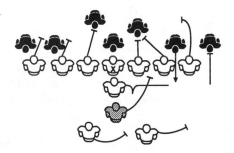 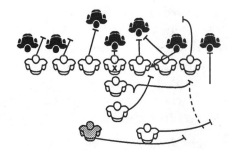

Wishbone formation triple option (defensive tackle has outside responsibility)

Wishbone triple option (defensive tackle has responsibility for the FB)

The triple option has the elements of finesse, power (because of the double team), and quickness. As such, it is very difficult to stop. The problem with the triple option is that, as the quarterback has to choose one of the two options in less than a half a second, there is ample opportunity for mistakes – the fullback may think he is keeping the ball, while the QB is trying to pull it away; the pitch may go astray; or the quarterback may make the wrong read. Also, because the true wishbone has three set backs, the pass isn't a serious threat to the defense.

Bill Yeoman at the University of Houston devised the veer or the Houston veer offense. He used two running backs to increase his passing threat by flanking a back and making use of a split end.

In the veer, the first option is to the diving halfback, rather than to the plunging fullback. The second option is to the offside halfback. In the wishbone, both halfbacks run wide, so that if the ball is pitched, the ball carrier has a lead blocker. In the veer, the halfback must go it alone, hoping that his fleetness of foot and his keenly intelligent fakes will help him elude his opponent.

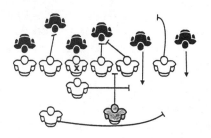

Veer option

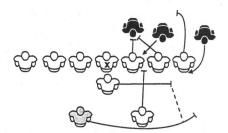

Option on the end (give to HB)

DEVELOPING THE PRIMARY RUNNING THREAT

Every play, with the exception of the quarterback sneak, is part of a series. The play series will be based on a power theory, a quickness theory, a finesse theory, or some combination of the three. In selecting a play series the coach must be guided by his overall theory of what he expects to do from that series. If he wants maximum power or finesse, having three backs in the backfield will probably be more effective. Does he want to pass? If so, he must have three or more immediate receivers next to the line of scrimmage, and he will probably want his running backs set wide so that they can get into the pass pattern quickly.

He may want his backfield action to yield a good faking action should he decide to pass. The Split T series would be a terrible series from which to pass because the wide line splits make it difficult to hold out the pass rushers, and the only immediate receivers are the ends. However, there are other series which will offer a good deal of faking and pass protection.

In theory, any back can hit any hole in the T-formation. However, in reality the fullback is a tough, hard-running and hard-blocking player, and the halfback is speedier and perhaps more elusive. Some coaches want a total power game and go with all backs playing like fullbacks. Others go with all halfbacks. Once in a while the coach is lucky enough to get a back who can do it all. Such a back makes the coach look like a genius.

PLAYS STARTING WITH THE FULLBACK THREAT

Many coaches will set up their basic attack with the fullback. He may buck at the guard and set up a cross buck or a belly series.

In the cross buck series, the fullback goes toward one of the guards. The halfback on that side then comes back either behind the QB or between the QB and the center. This is often done with the guard trap blocking.

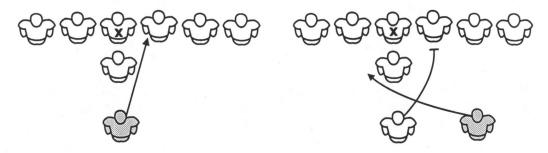

Fullback buck (straight blocking)   *Cross buck (straight ahead blocking)*

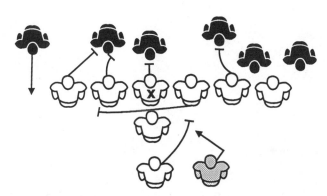

Cross buck (inside handoff, trap block)

Either cross buck can be done with straight ahead blocking or with a guard trapping while the fullback blocks the guard's man.

The fullback buck is also the beginning of the I formation isolation series, but the fullback is generally the lead blocker rather than the primary ball carrier.

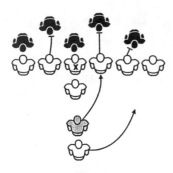

Buck from the I formation (QB open pivots)

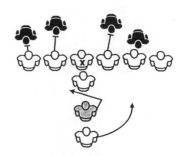

Fullback counter (buck) from I formation (QB reverse pivots)

Of course, when there is only one running back in the backfield, as in the A formation popularized by the Washington Redskins Coach Joe Gibbs with the running of John Riggins, that lone runner better be an animal.

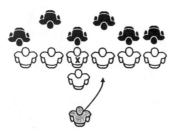

A formation buck

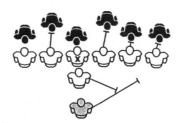

Slant

The slant play has the fullback going toward his tackle or end. This action is generally used as part of an outside play—the fullback either gets the ball as the primary runner, or he fakes and blocks while the halfback or quarterback goes wide.

- As part of the Split T series the fullback might get a cross block between the end and tackle or a double team by the end and tackle and an outside block by the diving halfback.

- As part of the quick pitch or fly series the quarterback fakes the pitch to the flying halfback, but gives to the fullback.

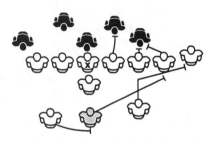

Split T slant

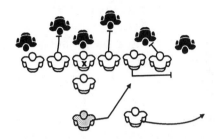

Fly series (quick pitch) slant

PLAYS STARTING WITH THE HALFBACK THREAT

The quick hitting halfback play is the dive. If the halfback is set behind the tackle, he will generally attack just inside or outside the tackle—often having the option, depending on how his tackle has blocked the opposing lineman. If he is set behind the guard, as in the veer, he will be able to attack from inside the guard to outside the tackle (the outside veer series).

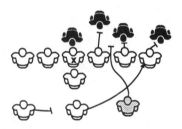

Dive play (defensive lineman blocked out)

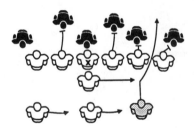

Dive play (defensive lineman blocked in)

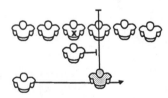

Inside veer (at guard)

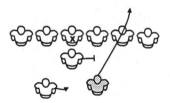

Outside veer (at tackle)

PLAYS WITH THE TAILBACK THREAT

When the coach calls the halfback a tailback, look out! It means that he is the primary ballcarrier. Whether it is the single wing, the double wing, or the I-formation—there's a guy back there ready to score. Whether it is Marcus Allen, Barry Sanders, or Herschel Walker in an I-formation, or Bruce Smith, Tom Harmon, or Paul Cameron in the single wing, you know that you have somebody back there who is either very fast, very powerful, or very tricky, and usually he is all three.

While some coaches believe that their offense is better served when they let their two or three running backs carry the ball in equal amounts, a theory which balances the attack, other coaches want their best man to carry the ball 80 or 90% of the time. In 1984, Auburn ran a wishbone with all the backs getting a chance to run the ball. One of those backs was Bo Jackson. When the 1985 season opened Auburn had changed its basic formation to the I formation, and Bo, as the tailback, got to run the ball all the way to the Heisman Trophy. John McKay had no problem in letting Heisman winners Marcus Allen or Mike Garrett carry the ball 30 or 40 times a game. As John said, "What's the problem? The ball's not heavy."

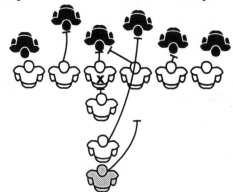

I formation – TB Blast

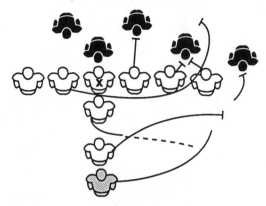

TB Power

THE BASIC RUNNING SERIES OF FOOTBALL

Certain series have become popular at different times during the evolution of the game. Often one part of a series will find its way into another series during a later period of that evolution.

The Tennessee single wing (balanced line) series includes the basic power play off tackle, the fullback buck, and the fullback spinner series with a possible reverse to the wingback or a handoff to the tailback.

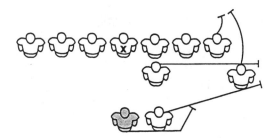

Off tackle power play (power)

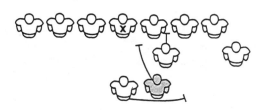

Fullback buck (power and quickness)

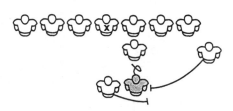

Spinner series (finesse)

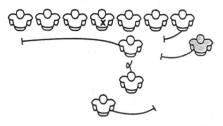

Reverse from spinner (finesse)

The unbalanced line single wing featured the basic off tackle and spinner series, but added what was probably the best finesse series in football. The Michigan teams of the late 1940s may have executed this series best. The buck-lateral series started with the ball being snapped to the fullback who would buck up the middle. The blocking back, instead of leading the play, turned around to face the fullback. The fullback could hand to the blocking back, who would then turn and run into the line, or he might drop back and pass, or he might hand to the wingback for a reverse, or most often he would lateral to the tailback who might then run wide or pass. This series threatened every hole.

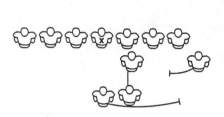

Buck lateral (possible reverse) finesse

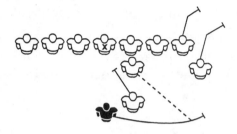

Buck lateral (run-pass option) finesse

The traditional tight-T or full house formation made possible quicker plays than did the single wing. The quick dives and bucks along with the threat of the immediate quick pass made this formation almost universal by the early 1950s.

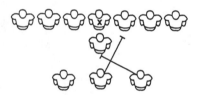

Buck-crossbuck

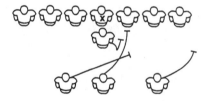

Inside belly series

Outside belly series – give to fullback

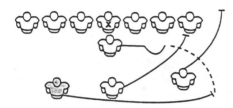

Option to halfback

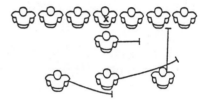

Dive

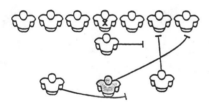

Fullback off tackle

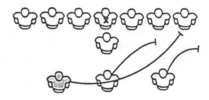

Halfback off tackle

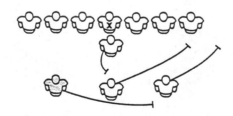

Halfback sweep

The Split T attack is based almost entirely on quickness, with only the FB counter as a finesse variation. The quarterback sneak is also an important part of the attack. Here is an illustrated basic SplitT series. Note that the line is split quite wide. The guard could split from one foot to six feet, the tackles two to eight feet, and the ends three to eight feet. The split depends on how far the defensive linemen will split with the offensive line. When a defensive lineman plays "head up" on any split, some coaches say "take them to the sidelines with your split."

Another advantage of the Split T quickness attack is that the fakes are done at the line of scrimmage. This means that each defender has to commit to the play in his area immediately and is therefore not able to pursue the play as quickly as he might be able to do when the fakes are deeper in the backfield.

The Split T series is based on the principle of creating lateral holes along the line of scrimmage by the split of the linemen with vertical holes resulting at every spot where there was a linebacker. Since the holes are already present when the team is lined up, all that the offensive lineman has to do is keep his defender in the same spot. He doesn't have to move him away from the hole as is necessary in the single wing.

Lateral and vertical holes resulting from line splits:

Dive, option series (quickness)   *Fullback counter (finesse)*

The Wing T developed by Dave Nelson at Delaware and made famous by Forest Evashevski at Iowa attempted to use much of the power of the single wing with the speed of the T or Split T.

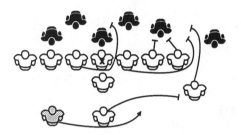

Off tackle power (backfield balanced)

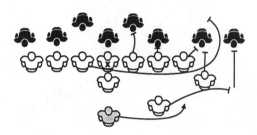

Off tackle power (strong set in backfield)

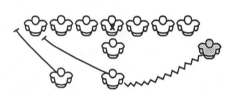

Off tackle power to wingback (who started in motion)

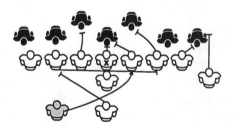

Crossbuck action or tackle trap

John McKay's Pro I attack incorporated much of the power of the single wing and some of the quickness of the T, with the passing potential of the professional wide formation. While the fullback buck and the outside belly series were integral parts of the attack, he added the isolation play for power and a new idea of option running for his talented tailbacks. If the linemen just stayed with the defenders, the tailback could pick his holes. He might run to where the play was designed to go, or he might run wider or cutback.

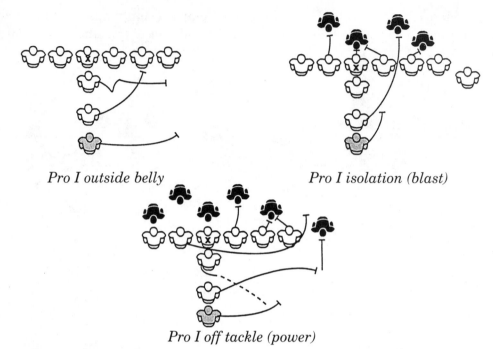

Pro I outside belly   *Pro I isolation (blast)*

Pro I off tackle (power)

You can see that coaches have a great many options from which to choose in developing a running attack. They can't have it all. Each coach must choose whether to emphasize a power, quickness, or finesse attack. He must then decide whether he is going to feature one primary ball carrier or spread the ball carrying responsibilities and balance his attack. He must decide whether to fit the players to his system or fit a system to his players – changing every year or so. Or he may take a primary system and fit the players to his system – making small changes each year to accommodate his current players' talents – emphasizing a tough fullback one year and a fast halfback the next.

The number of running plays possible are countless. The problem is that there isn't enough time to teach all possible plays to each team. Some coaches have tried to mix formations using a "multiple offense." Biggie Munn did it at Michigan State. He used the T, wing T, single and double wing – 14 different backfield sets in all.

7
BLOCKING FOR THE RUNNING PLAY

It's a lot easier to draw up a backfield series than it is to make it work on the field. What makes it work is the blocking pattern and the skills of the blockers.

Coaches often argue as to which is the most important segment of a football team. Some coaches hold that it is the defensive corner backs, but most hold that it is the offensive line. The media hype the so called "skilled positions"—the quarterback, running backs, receivers and defensive backs. But you better believe that the offensive line is all-important!

Can you visualize the Seahawk offensive line going against a bunch of ten-year-olds on a Pop Warner team? You can bet that your 90 year old grandmother as quarterback could score a touchdown on every play.

On the other hand, if you put Barry Sanders or Marshall Faulk behind that Pop Warner offensive line against the Seahawk defense, they wouldn't gain a yard if they played two games a day for the rest of this century.

You may have heard about the time that Knute Rockne's famous backfield, called the "Four Horsemen," was getting a bit cocky because of all the publicity they had received. So, in one game Rockne took out the Seven Mules—the nickname for the first string Notre Dame line. To the surprise of the Horsemen, they were totally ineffective. Only when the "mules" were inserted in the game did the starting backs start to run with abandon. The old coach had taught a great lesson in humility.

It is no small wonder that great backs appreciate their offensive lines. Most great running backs take good care of the men who have taken care of them. Expensive gifts and sumptuous dinners are the small price that these appreciative backs pay to the players who make them look so good.

DESIGNING THE BLOCKING SCHEMES

Running and passing plays have blocking rules for every lineman and usually for some of the backs. The coach who develops the rules for each play must take into consideration the multitude of possibilities in defensive alignments. Following are some common defensive alignments:

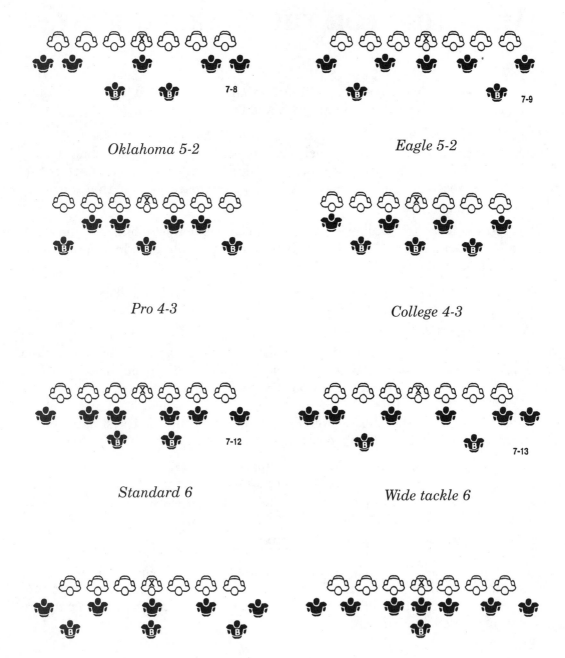

Oklahoma 5-2   *Eagle 5-2*

Pro 4-3   *College 4-3*

Standard 6   *Wide tackle 6*

5-3   *7 diamond*

Sometimes linebackers are stacked behind a lineman (as in the 5-3 or 7 diamond above). In other situations, they are stacked in a gap. A gap stack presents some real problems in blocking, especially with a one-on-one blocking scheme—where one offensive player must block one defensive player without the help of a team mate in a double team block.

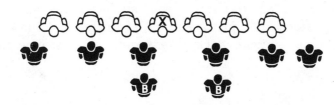

A defense using two gap stacks

Many defenses put linemen or linebackers in the gaps, or put them on the inside or outside shoulder of an offensive lineman, giving the defender the gap responsibility. The gap placement or gap responsibility is needed to reduce the splits of the offensive linemen.

Split 6 alignment   *Gap 8*

Oklahoma 5-2 with tackles and ends having outside shades

BLOCKING RULES

Running plays based on quickness often have very simple rules. Here are some simple systems:

Number blocking. The center takes the 0 man (the man over him). The guard takes the number 1 man (first man away from the center on his side. The tackle takes the number 2 man. The end takes the number 3 man, and the first back out of the backfield might take the 4th man. Against an Oklahoma 5-2, it works very simply. Against a "man stack," you just assume that the stacked linebacker is one hole closer to the play. Against a gap stack, this type of rule has some problems.

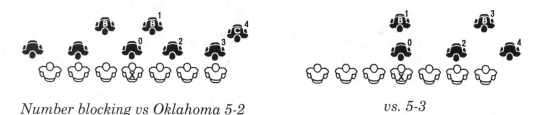

Number blocking vs Oklahoma 5-2   *vs. 5-3*

Versus a gap stack, the coach might assume that the stack is lined up on the man inside or outside.

Actual alignment   *Assumed alignment*

*Assumed — If the coach decides to block
it as if it were on the next man out it
would be blocked this way.*

Another good rule of thumb, applicable when a team is trapping the outside of the hole, is "take the man on or the first man away from the hole." If there is a gap stack just assume that the stack is on the next man in.

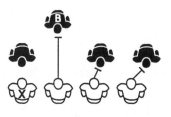

vs. Oklahoma 5-2

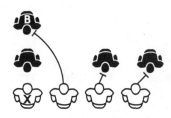

vs. 5-3

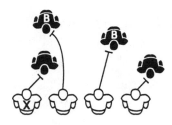

vs. gap stack

For wide plays, this rule can be changed to "take the man on or the first man toward the hole."

vs. gap 8

vs. a gap stack

A very common approach to making blocking rules is giving a priority of assignments which can take care of every situation. Each play will have a different rule. Here is a sample of rules used by many wishbone teams. This is called base blocking or the basic blocking rule.

- Center—man on, playside gap, first man downfield

- Guard to play side—block first man on the line of scrimmage who is inside your tackle.

- Playside tackle—block first man head up or to your inside (whether he is on of off the line of scrimmage)

- Playside end—block safety in 4 deep, defensive halfback (corner back) in a 3 deep secondary alignment.

- Offside guard—block first man to your side of the center (whether he is on or off the line of scrimmage)

- Offside tackle—seal first man outside guard and block the second man on your side of the center. (Seal means get in front of him so that he has to go behind you—before you make your block.)

Many teams have a basic blocking rule which will work against most defenses, then have special rules for certain plays. This basic blocking rule is called "base" blocking.

Here is a typical base blocking rule which is applicable on most plays for the center, play side guard, tackle, and end. The rule is: inside gap, man on, first man downfield. This means that the lineman must first check the gap to his inside. If there is a man there, he blocks him. His next responsibility is to block the man on him. If neither of these situations applies, he should block the first man downfield (possibly a linebacker or defensive back).

CALLING THE BLOCKS ON THE LINE OF SCRIMMAGE

Often the linemen, usually the guards, are allowed to call how they will block a given play. They will use code words or letters. Usually every man on the line will call out a word, but the only one that counts is the key man on that particular play. The key man may be the man on the inside or the outside of the hole. This takes a great deal of intelligence to see the alignment, anticipate the stunts, determine where the play should hit, then call the proper block—all in about 3 to 5 seconds. No wonder the offensive guards score the highest on the intelligence tests given by the NFL. (Quarterbacks are second.)

Some teams will label each block with a letter. Here is a traditional use of letters for calling the blocking:

A (basic rule)

B cross block (outside man goes first)

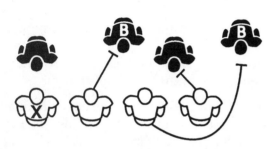

B blocking with the inside man blocking a linebacker (usually called a "fold" block).

C cross block (inside man goes first) With outside man "folding" on linebacker

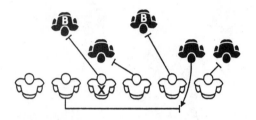 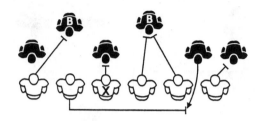

Trap with linemen blocking down   *Trap with double team*

The trap block was first called the mouse trap. In the old days when all linemen charged hard into the backfield, one man would often be unblocked and coaxed into a mousetrap where the pulling guard could easily block him. Modern defensive techniques have made this a more difficult block to make, but it is still often used.

Some teams have a code word when they want to exchange blocking assignments. Only the two men at the hole are involved. Perhaps the inside man says "me," meaning that he will go first. If he says "you," he means that his partner will block first while the man calling the block will go behind. If the key man doesn't want to exchange assignments he might say "go," meaning to go ahead with the basic rule for that play. (Remember that all the linemen are saying "me" "you," or "go.")

One-on-one blocking at the hole between the guard and tackle versus an Oklahoma 5-2 could be done these three ways if only the guard and tackle are involved.

"Go" call   *"Me" call*

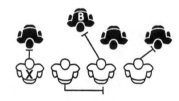

"You" call

Instead of a "me" or "you" call, the coach might decide to use a more variable code. An example might be for the inside man to call any city—meaning that he will go first. So whether he says Dallas, Baltimore, San Francisco, or Paris—it all means the same thing. Similarly, if he wants the outside man to go first, he might call any color. Therefore, whenever a coach refers to a cross block with the inside man going first (whether in a practice, chalk talk, play book or game), he refers to it as a "city" block. Whenever he refers to a cross block with the outside man going first, he refers to it as a "color" block.

Most coaches will use codes for blocking rules, formations, play patterns, pass defense coverages, defensive stunts, and automatics. Often they develop their own secret codes. Other times they borrow codes from famous coaches. In football, you can't keep anything secret for long.

Today's blocking schemes have become more and more complicated. No longer are the guards the only linemen who pull and trap, and no longer are traps only from the inside of the formation to the outside.

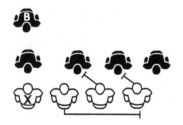 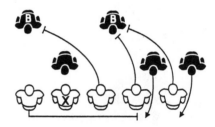

Traditional traps (mousetraps)

While the guard is still the primary pulling and trapping lineman on most teams, and while the inside out trap is the most common type of trap, today the center, tackles, ends, wingbacks, or the man in motion can all pull and perhaps trap.

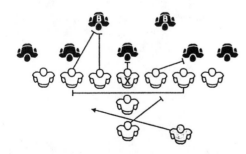 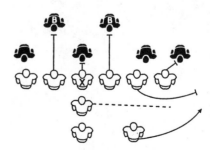

Tackle trapping in a counter   *Tackle pulling on a quick pitch*

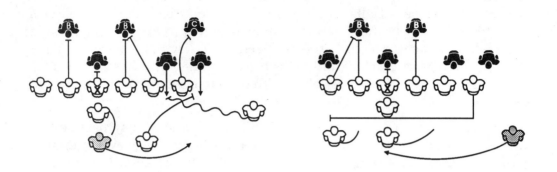

Back in motion trapping   *End trapping on reverse*

Using the backs to block is an integral part of most offenses today. There used to be ten blockers and a tailback who got all the glory. The single wing series, which is mentioned in the last chapter, is the ultimate in using the backs as blockers.

The old T-formation plays and the Split T attacks relied more on quickness and finesse rather than power blocking, so the backs were not often used as primary blockers.

But today with the I pro, the power I and the wing T running attacks, as well as the emphasis on pass protection for the quarterback, it is imperative that the backs (especially the I formation fullback) be effective blockers.

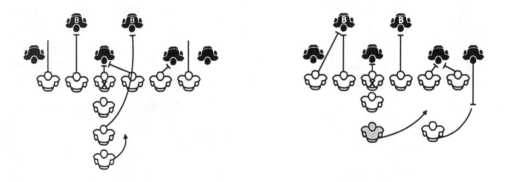

Pro I isolation block lead   *Off tackle with the halfback*

DOWNFIELD BLOCKING

It isn't enough to block the defenders near the point of attack. Nearly every play in modern football is designed to score a touchdown. This requires that some linemen be released downfield in front of the ball carrier.

If the play is in the center of the line, both ends will usually be released. It is possible that one or both tackles will also release downfield.

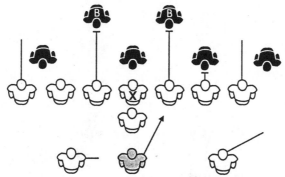

Fullback buck with ends releasing

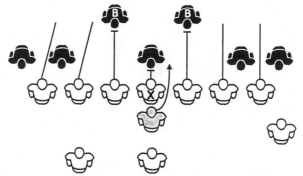

QB sneak with tackles and ends releasing

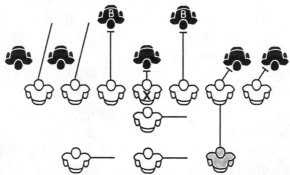

A dive right with left tackle and end releasing

A LOOK AT SOME TOTAL BLOCKING PATTERNS

Here are several ways that a fullback slant can be blocked against an Oklahoma 5-2:

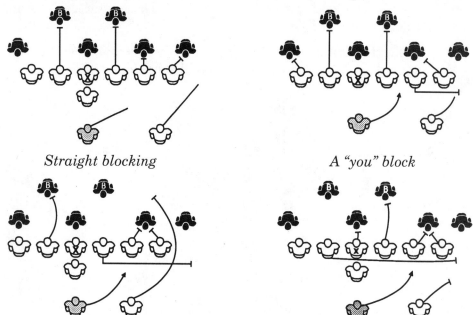

Straight blocking   *A "you" block*

*A double team with onside guard trap-
ping*   *Double team with offside guard trapping*

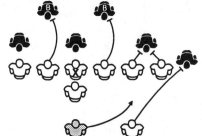

Double team with halfback blocking out

With these five simple ways to block one play against one defense, just imagine the possibilities for blocking this one play against the nine defenses illustrated early in the chapter. Keep in mind that there are many more defensive alignments than we illustrated and there are several ways to block any one play. This is where the X's and O's that the coaches play with become so complicated.

In fact, one of the coach's major jobs is to determine which blocking schemes will probably work best against the next opponent's probable defenses. Since we don't have 50 hours a day to practice, we are greatly limited in our ability to meet every possibility with which our next opponent will confront us. That's why every play doesn't work on the field like it does in our playbooks.

8

PASSING THEORY

Many people think that the forward pass is the heart of the game. While passing plays are often the most exciting, and the fans pay to see the "big plays," most coaches see it as a necessary, but fascinating, accessory to the real essentials of the game—defense, running, and kicking.

The forward pass is a cornerstone of the pro attack and the delight of the fans. While teams which play the best defense and teams that can run the ball are statistically the most likely to win, the passing game is a necessity winning—especially at the professional level. The skill of the passers and receivers makes it much more likely that a pass in a professional game will be complete than a pass in a high school game. Still, even at the high school level a team must have an effective passing attack in order to take advantage of whatever weaknesses the defense gives them.

It is hard to believe that this present day phenomenon was once a lowly orphan in the game. It wasn't even legal until 36 years after the game was invented. Some pressure on the rules committee by such coaches as Eddie Cochems of St. Louis University and John Heisman at Clemson College (the man after whom the Heisman trophy is named) resulted in Walter Camp, the head of the football rules committee, legalizing the forward pass in 1906. A few years later Camp tried to have it again ruled illegal because he wanted to increase the running game's effectiveness.

In the movie *Knute Rockne, All American*, Pat O'Brien as Knute was shown practicing the pass during the summer months at Cedar Point in Ohio. Then several months later he sprung the surprise of all times on the heavily favored Army team as little Notre Dame from the west defeated the Cadets. It really did happen that way, but the pass had been used by teams in the midwest since St. Louis completed the first pass against Carroll College in early September of 1906 and Wesleyan completed a against a mighty Yale team on October 3, 1906. But the big rough house teams of the East weren't ready for the "sissy" pass so it remained for the teams from the midwest and the south to develop it.

In those days, the ball was still somewhat like a blimp—like a rugby ball, so it was very hard to throw. So the first passes were more like basketball chest passes or were thrown underhand end over end. However, it didn't take players long to learn how to throw the overhand spiral. In fact Bradbury Robinson of St. Louis University was credited with several 50-yard pass completions in 1906.

Much of the credit for the early development of the pass is given to Eddie Cochems. However, Pop Warner at Carlisle Institute, Amos Alonzo Stagg of The University of Chicago, and Jesse Harper, Rockne's coach at Notre Dame, are all considered among the pioneers in the development of the forward pass.

The rules relating to the pass have changed a bit over the years. At first the passer had to throw from a spot at least 5 yards deep and 5 yards to the side of where the ball was snapped and an incomplete pass cost the throwing team a 15-yard penalty. In 1910 it was made illegal to pass more than 20 yards downfield —because the pass was taking away from the "real game" of football. This rule lasted only two years. Also in 1910, the passer was no longer required to pass from 5 yards wide of the center, but he still had to be 5 yards deep when he threw.

The shape of the ball was changed in 1931 to make it easier to throw. And by 1934 the rule requiring a 5-yard penalty for the second incomplete pass in a series was eliminated. By 1941 the rule which required that a pass which fell incomplete in the end zone was ruled as a touchback and went over to the other team was eliminated. By 1945 it was made legal to pass from anywhere behind the line of scrimmage. The last major change was to allow any back less than a yard behind the line (such as the T-formation quarterback) to be eligible. This was passed as recently as 1963. So you see the forward pass has had an Horatio Alger history—from orphan to millionaire status.

It may seem to some spectators that all the coach has to worry about is getting the receivers open. It's like the old days in the park when we were kids and Charlie would tell Joey to "Go out and hide behind the tree and I'll throw you a long one." That theory worked great in pick-up games after school in the third grade. Today it is just a bit more complicated.

The passing game is an essential part of any offensive plan of attack. While the running game allows a team to attack the width of the field, the passing game allows the offensive team to attack both the width and the depth of field.

For a team in which the run is primary, the formations chosen will tend to be tight—four backs and two tight ends.

Tight T formation   *Single wing*

Wing T

In order to develop the threat of the pass, a running team may split one end or flank one back to widen the area which the defense must protect.

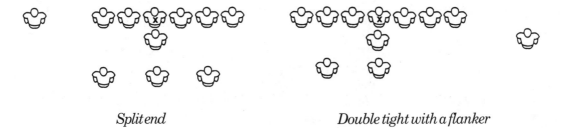

Split end   *Double tight with a flanker*

Teams looking for a balanced attack are more likely to split two people in order to develop a more immediate passing threat.

Split end and flanker (Pro set)

Split end and slot back

The teams which plan on relying largely on the pass will often place three, four, or even five people in positions where they can release immediately for the pass.

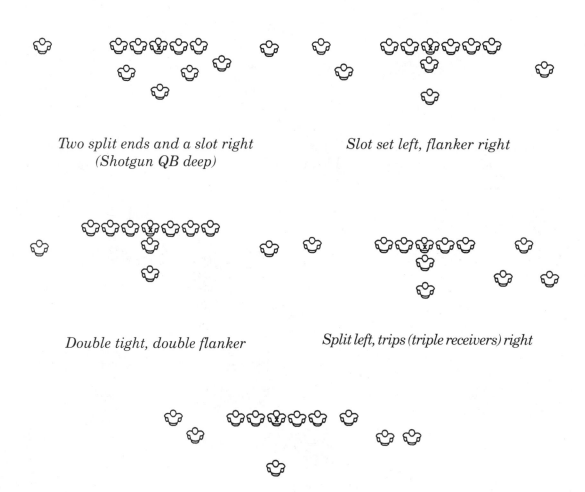

Two split ends and a slot right
(Shotgun QB deep)

Slot set left, flanker right

Double tight, double flanker

Split left, trips (triple receivers) right

Slot left, trips right

Some coaches see the pass as their primary attack. Safe passes which are short, but give the potential for long runs after the catch, have been used by the 49ers for years. Brigham Young University has achieved a great deal of fame, and a national title, with this theory. More recently the run and shoot offense developed by Glenn "Tiger" Ellison and popularized by Mouse Davis at Portland State and the Detroit Lions has centered around the pass. Houston has had considerable success with this scheme.

Teams using the forward pass want to stretch the defense vertically and horizontally. They want to be able to hit out patterns right on the sidelines and they want to be able to throw the 60 yard pass deep. Once they have established that they can do both of these things the defensive team must be prepared to defense the whole field.

The Great Wall of China or the Maginot Line of France might well have stopped an infantry and cavalry in their day, but neither would be able to stop today's air forces or helicopter warfare. So the gap 8 or goal line defenses may be effective against a pure running team but they are very vulnerable to the pass.

A passing attack of some sort is essential for every football team, just as every army needs an air force. Every defense must be constantly on guard against the pass—which often opens up the run.

THE ACTION OF THE PASSER

The most common type of pass is the "drop back" pass. The quarterback either backpedals or turns and runs to a set depth before setting up to pass. Dropback passes are designed for the quarterback to drop one, three, five, seven and sometimes nine steps. His depth depends on the depth that the receiver is to run in his route.

The passer who turns and runs to his passing spot can get back quicker. But the passer who backpedals is better able to see what the defense is doing and read the defense more effectively.

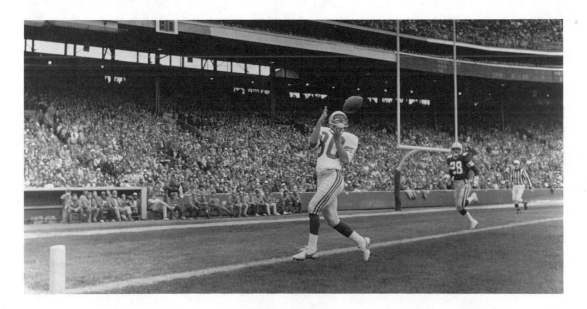

Steve Largent

Play action passes are another type of passing action. In this type of action the quarterback fakes a running play then sets to pass. This action usually holds the linebackers and opens up the underneath zones effectively. If the line blocks aggressively, as they would do on a running play, the defensive backs may also be fooled. But with aggressive blocking they may not be able to give the quarterback effective protection. If, however, they do their normal pass protection blocking (standing up and retreating) they will generally not fool the defensive backs.

Pocket protection

When the quarterback is in a rollout action, he runs deep behind the protection of his backs. He may pass from ten to twenty yards wider than he lined up. This rolling action puts a great deal of pressure on the defensive player who is assigned to cover the short wide area and to support on a wide running play. If the defender drops to protect for the pass, the quarterback may be able to run; if the defender comes up to support the run, the pass is open. Many teams use the option available in this situation to read the defensive corner then make the play. Just as in a running option play in which the quarterback options the defensive end or linebacker and pitchs back to a trailing back, in the pass option he reads the defensive force man and runs or passes forward.

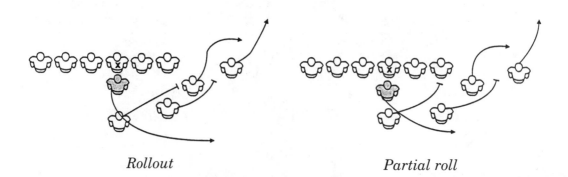

Rollout   *Partial roll*

The partial roll out starts as a full roll but the quarterback pulls up. The movement of the quarterback past the offensive tackle will often signal the defense to change their assignments with a wide pass defender having to move up to support the possible run. This may open up another man in the pass pattern. As the defenders rotate their pass coverage and change their zone responsibilities, the throwback pass may open up.

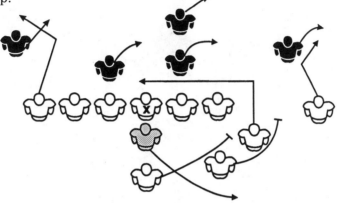

Partial roll with throwback open

If the coach wants a quicker pressure on the defensive flat area he may use the sprint out pass. The sprint out pass is similar to the roll, but it is faster and more shallow so it puts quicker pressure on the defensive cornerback to make up his mind as to whether to play the run or the pass. The sprint out is similar to the option play discussed in the chapter on running theory. But while in the option play the QB can run or pitch back, in the sprint out he can run or pitch forward. There is much more of a run threat than in the deeper rollout.

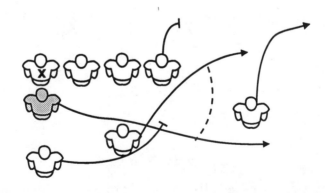

Sprint out pass

The moving pocket (rove or controlled scramble) is a more recent development. Joe Gibbs of the Redskins developed an action which started as a drop back pass, then it looked like Joe Theisman was scrambling out of the pocket—but the whole action was planned. Joe Montana also used this action as a way to clear himself from the pass rushers.

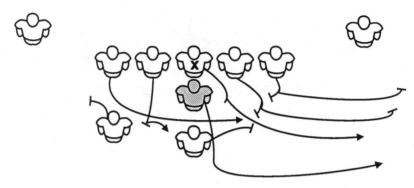

Rove

The bootleg is like a rollout, but it is away from the flow of the backs. The QB will fake to a back and keep the ball, going the opposite direction. He may or may not have a pulling lineman to block for him. This play is highly effective on the goal line or in short yardage situations in which everybody but the quarterback has a man assigned to guard him.

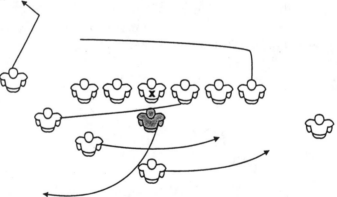

Boot with flood pattern

Play action passes are especially important to teams which rely on the run. Some teams will have the linemen perform the normal retreat pass protection, others will block aggressively as if the play is a run. The aggressive blocking is more likely to fool the defensive backs who are often keying the linemen—but the passer will probably not be protected as long.

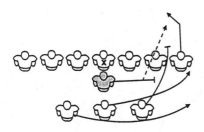

Split T dive pass

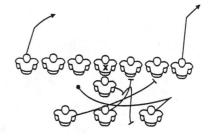

Belly counter pass

PROTECTING THE PASSER

Probably the most important part of the passing attack is the protection of the passer. There is no question that you can't have a good passing attack unless the passer can get his pass off. And the more time he has, the more effective he will be. Consequently, the blocking schemes which an offensive line must learn in a sophisticated passing attack are quite complicated.

There is an old coaching maxim that you should rush the good passer but cover the poor passer, because of the chance of interception—so the better the passer, the more a coach must teach pass protection.

As an example, let's take a simple "man" blocking scheme. The player is responsible for the defensive man who lines up on him. Here is how it would look in an Oklahoma 5-2 or the pro 3-4 with the linebackers reacting back as the passer "shows" pass by dropping back.

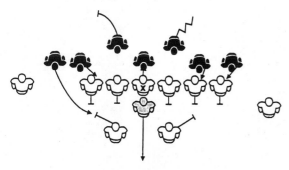

Oklahoma 5-2

Pro 3-4

If the linebackers rush straight, which they seldom do, it would look like this in a pro 3-4 and pro 4-3.

Pro 3-4   *Pro 4-3*

Big on big is another type of man blocking. Here you have the linemen responsible for the defensive linemen rather than the man on. The center takes the "0" man, the guard the "1" man and the tackle the "2" man. In a pro 4-3 it is quite simple, the guards and tackles take the men on them and the center drops back to help where needed—assuming that his linebacker doesn't rush. The backs in this scheme would be responsible for the linebackers should they rush the passer.

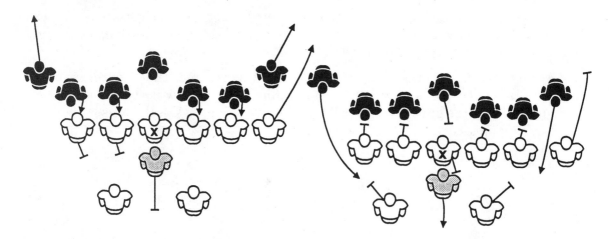

Pro 4-3 linebacker drops   *Pro 4-3 linebacker rushes*

Here is how it would look against a wide tackle 6 and a pro 3-4.

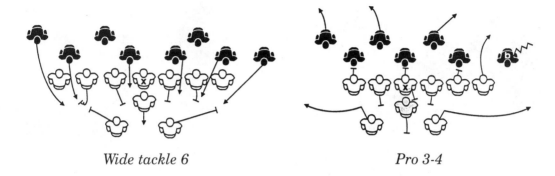

Wide tackle 6   *Pro 3-4*

Quite often the backs will be assigned to block if they see the linebackers rushing, but they may be allowed to swing to the outside if the linebackers drop back.

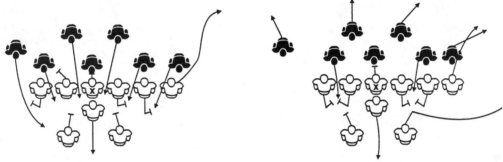

Pro 3-4 linebackers rush   *Pro 3-4 linebackers drop*

If the defense decides that they really want to sack the passer, here is what is most likely to happen. (Defenses and the theories of stunting will be more thoroughly discussed in the chapters on defense. Meanwhile just sit back and be as confused as offensive coordinators are when their pass protection breaks down and their quarterbacks wonder why they aren't playing pro golf instead of pro football.)

Possible stunt from pro 4-3

Full rush with safety blitz

Possible stunt from a 5-3

A stunt from a 3-4

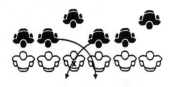

Tackles twist

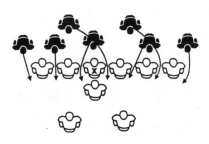

Okie

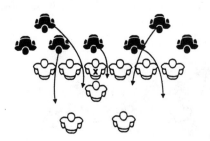

Eagle

Okie stunt to an eagle

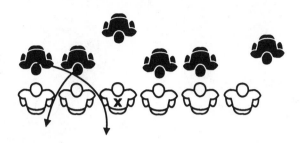

Tackle and end twist in 4-3

It looks relatively simple on paper, but on the field it is murder.

Slide protection is another type of adjustment which a team may make. If an offensive lineman is having trouble blocking his man, the coach might get him help by sliding another man over to help him. If the protection is slide left, and help is needed on the nose tackle, the right guard will check to make certain that his linebacker is not rushing. If not, he is free to slide to his left and help the center on the noseguard.

Slide protection

In order to take away the advantage of the defenders switching positions in a stunt or a twist, another blocking scheme which can be used is a "zone." In a "zone" scheme the blocker sets up and waits to see who comes into his area. It might be the man who lined up on him, but it might well be somebody else. Here are some possibilities.

Stunt from 4-3   *Stunt from 3-4 with a safety blitz*

You always hope that your quarterback can see this all happening and dump off the ball to a tight end or a back. But quarterbacks have many other things to worry about, such as:"Are they going to knock me down and get my uniform dirty?," or "How much should I ask for in my next contract negotiation," or "Where does my girl friend want to eat tonight?"

PASS PATTERNS

Pass patterns can be individual routes or team patterns. They may have names or numbers. Most coaches will develop a "passing tree" in which the most common patterns are numbered. Commonly the patterns were designed to break from the line of scrimmage, at 5 yards, and at 10 yards. But as coaches have become more adept at designing patterns to beat where the defenders were more likely to be, the depth of the patterns has changed.

At the pro level, where defenses change from play to play, a pattern is not exact. If the defense rotates into one zone the receiver may cut the pattern shorter or make it longer. If the defense has switched to a man-to-man defense, requires receivers to make other adjustments.

Generally against a zone defense the receiver will try to get to an open area then stop and wait for the ball. But against a man defense he will make sharp cuts or lean into the defender then break off. Since the passer is reading the same defenders as the receiver, the passer has a good idea as to how the receiver will run his route.

In high school, most linebackers are taught to drop back to a 10-yard depth. Consequently, passing coaches often have their patterns break at 7 yards (in front of the backers), at 13 yards (just behind the backers, where the receivers can easily slide between the backers), and at 18 yards (safely behind the backers). At the college and professional levels, the routes may break deeper than 20 yards.

The types of patterns which the coach will choose to run will be determined by the expected defenses. Theoretically there are six short zones and three deep zones. But coaches almost never commit nine players to these zones and rush only two defenders, so we commonly think in terms of three deep and four shallow zones.

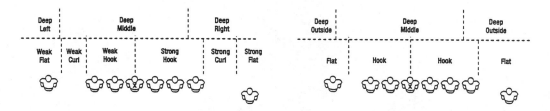

Theoretical model of six shallow and three deep zones

Often used three deep-four shallow zones

With today's great passers and adept receivers, teams which play only these seven zones are easier to attack so coaches will often change the pass coverage from down to down. Among the common coverages are a five under zone with two deep backs, a five under man-to-man coverage with two deep safeties, a five under three deep zone, a man-to-man defense with one safety, and a pure man to man coverage.

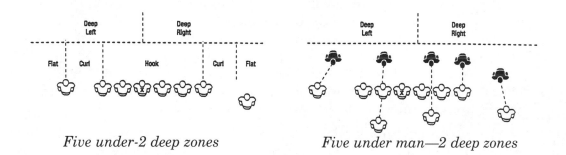

Five under-2 deep zones

Five under man—2 deep zones

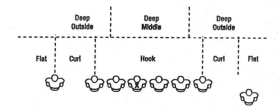

Five under -3 deep zones

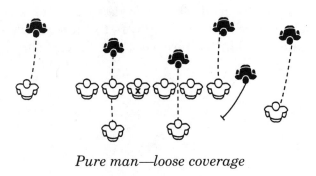

Pure man—loose coverage

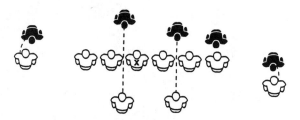

Pure man—tight coverage

CALLING THE ROUTES

Pass patterns have names which describe their actions. A "flag" or "corner" route is designed to have the receiver going deep and out towards the marker (which used to be a flag) at the front corner of the end zone. A "post" was the designation of the pattern designed to go long and in—towards the goal posts. A "buttonhook" or "hook" pattern looked like a buttonhook when drawn on the blackboard. A "spot" pass had the receiver staying in the same spot where he lined up. And an "out" or "sideline" pattern had the receiver going toward the sideline—and usually coming back slightly toward the line of scrimmage, to get away from the defensive back.

As more patterns were developed and passing offenses became more sophisticated, many coaches numbered the patterns. If the patterns were overlaid upon each other they looked something like a tree. By using numbers in progression of short to long passes the coaches could more easily teach more patterns.

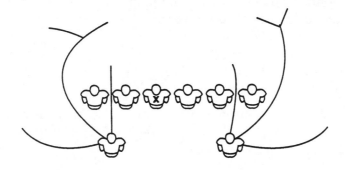

Left side patterns   *Right side patterns*

SAMPLE OF A PASSING TREE
(note that even numbers are inside patterns, odds are out)

Some backfield patterns

Assuming that the coach is using the passing tree numbers, he might call the split end (usually called the X receiver), the tight end (the Y man), or the flanker or slot (the Z man) as the primary pass receiver. The other receivers might run "complementary" patterns.

For example if the coach calls a Y-9 or a Y corner, the tight end should run deep to the corner of the field, the other two receivers should know what to run. Perhaps the nearest other receiver knows that he should run an intermediate level pattern in the same line of sight as the Y receiver, and the other receiver might have been told to run a short pattern in the line of sight area. This would give what is called a vertical stretch of the defense—three men in the same line with each one at different levels.

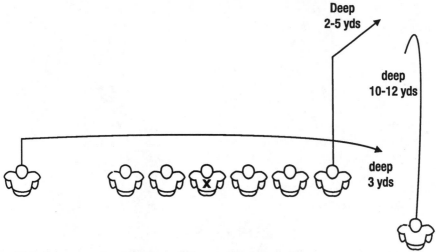

Y-9 (or corner) with X and Z running complementary patterns

Often the coach wants to totally control the pattern and wants to take the guess work out of the minds of the players, so he might call 493—meaning the X runs a four, the Y runs a nine, and the Z runs a three. This would give the same effect as the pattern explained in the above paragraph, but would be more explicit. But the quarterback may not be as aware of his primary receiver when the coach calls a 493 so he has to look for the open receiver. When the coach called Y-9, the quarterback had a pretty good idea of who the coach thought would be open.

Another type of complementary pattern would be all receivers running hooks (two patterns) or curls (3 patterns). This would give a horizontal stretch—with all of the players at the same depth across the field.

Y-2

Obviously some patterns work better against some defenses. A fast halfback has the advantage over a slower linebacker if the coverage is man-to-man. Deep curl patterns (at 18 to 23 yards) would work against most zone coverages. Sending three players deep against a two deep zone may work. But since coverages are generally disguised, the offensive team is never quite sure what defense will develop as the quarterback drops to pass.

Team patterns are often called to put some special pressure on the defense. In a flood pattern the offense tries to flood one area with more receivers than can be covered by the defense.

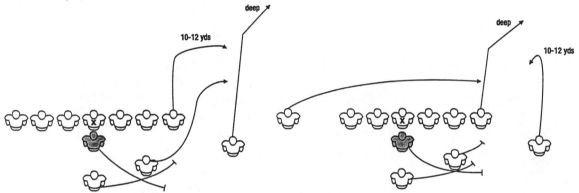

Two roll out passes flooding the right zones

GETTING THE RECEIVER OPEN

Many coaches will attempt to get their best receiver against the poorest defender on the defense. They put the best or fastest wide outs against the poorest or slowest cornerbacks and their fastest running back against the slowest linebacker. This certainly gives the offense a "leg up" on getting a man open.

If the receiver is being bumped by a defender he must first get free of him. He may use a head fake, he may fake a block on the defender then get into his pattern, he may spin away from the defender, or he may use his arms to knock the arms of the defender away. Once he is free of the defender's bumping he may attack a defensive back. Some coaches teach the receiver to run a straight line to the place where he will make his cut, others approach the defender in a weave.

Some coaches teach a hard right angle cut. A receiver who wants to cut right will plant his left foot and drive hard to the right. Sometimes, especially on deeper routes, the receiver will make a double cut. And some coaches teach a rounded cut. The rounded cut gets the player wider faster, but doesn't fool the defender as much. However, if the receiver can get close to the defender and make the defender turn and run with him, then make his turn when the defender has his legs crossed, he can increase the distance between himself and the defender.

Square cut   *Weave and rounded cut*

Against man-to-man coverage making good cuts or making the cut at the proper time is particularly important. If a team is playing a zone defense, the defenders should be paying more attention to being in the proper place on the field in relation to the ball than to the cut of the receivers. So receivers are often less concerned about faking a defender than they are about getting to an open area between the zones.

USING THE PASS TO ATTACK THE DEFENSE

There are so many ways a defense can cover a pass on any given play that the quarterbacks and receivers must learn to "read" the defenses.

The passer and receivers must first answer the question of whether the coverage is a regular man-for-man (with the defensive backs five to 10 yards off the line), a bump and run man-for-man or zone. If it is man-for-man, the best patterns are comebacks (sidelines, hooks, curls); fakes, especially double fakes (Z out or in, hook and go, out and up); or patterns in which the receiver can get the defender to turn and run one way then, just as he crosses his legs, cut behind him. This makes it very difficult for the defender to recover in time to stop the pass. Versus bump and run the receiver may lean into the defender then make a break, he may run some sort of a comeback pattern, or he may simply try to outrun him.

When it is quite certain that the defense will be in a man-to-man defense, crossing receivers are often effective in screening out the defenders. One such type of pattern is a pick play similar to those common in basketball. Just as in basketball, moving picks are illegal. But if a player hooks and stops and somehow gets in the way of a defender covering another player, it is legal. Such plays are often used on the goal line where man to man coverage is common.

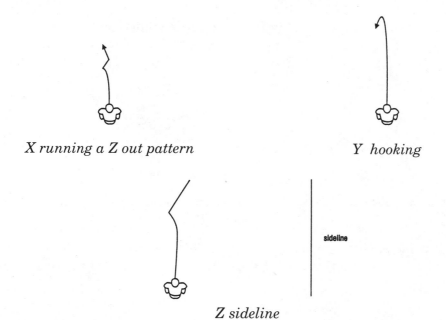

X running a Z out pattern

Y hooking

sideline

Z sideline

PATTERNS WHICH ARE EFFECTIVE AGAINST A MAN DEFENSE

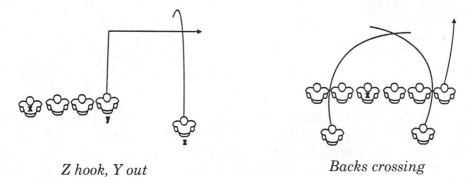

Z hook, Y out

Backs crossing

Pick plays

When the team uses a lot of zone covers, as most teams do, patterns can be called in the huddle and the read is relatively simple.

Here is a pattern, often called orbit, in which the defender being read is the man responsible for the flat area.

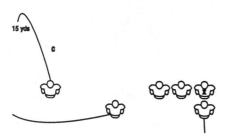

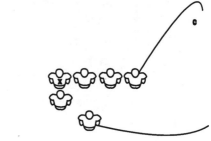

Orbit pattern with split end and slot back

Orbit pattern with tight end and running back

This same principle can be used on any short zone defender with a man curling deep and another at about a five yards beyond the line of scrimmage.

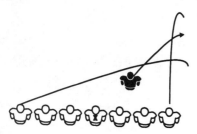

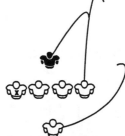

Two tight ends in one inside backer's zone

A tight end and a back in an inside backer's zone

Most teams play four defensive backs, but need to cover only three deep zones. One of the defenders can be freed to cover a flat zone to the strong side. (The strong side can be the side to which the ball rolls, the wide side of the field, or the side of the two receivers.) If the cornerback is assigned to cover the flat it is often called cloud coverage. If the safety is assigned the flat for that play it is often called sky coverage. "C" stands for corner and cloud, "S" for safety and sky.

Cloud cover to two receiver side

Sky cover to two receiver side

When a coach knows that an opponent will be using only two or three defensive adjustments he may develop a simple read to help the quarterback and receivers find an opening. Here is a common read used against teams which use cloud and sky covers. It is called a post-read pattern. While the wide receiver starts to run a post pattern, both he and the quarterback watch the safety. If the safety starts wider and deep, the receiver changes his pattern to a corner and is ahead of the safety. If the safety starts wide but does not get depth it means that he will be covering the flat so the cornerback will have the deep third of the field. In this case the receiver breaks inside the cornerback and runs a post pattern. The passer must get the ball to him quickly so that the other safety who is now moving to the deep middle zone cannot react to the ball. If it turns out that the defense is in man-to-man coverage, the receiver breaks back toward the passer after he has run about 15-yards downfield.

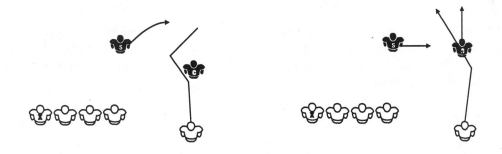

Post-read, safety has deep outside zone (cloud)

Post-read, safety covers flat (sky)

Another type of read occurs when an offensive player assigned to watch a linebacker sees the backer stunting. This means that his zone has been vacated. That offensive receiver yells "hot" and runs to the area. The QB passes immediately—no matter what pattern had been called in the huddle. Some teams will make the strong linebacker the first read so they don't have to yell "hot," they just read it.

Tight end as hot receiver

Tight end blocking if linebacker plays "honest"

More complicated reads can involve looking at two or three defenders to determine the coverage. Usually there is an alignment key and a movement key.

Here is an example of a mirrored pattern, that is, the routes are the same on both sides of the line of scrimmage. The prime targets are the X and Z men. If the outs are covered, the running backs should be open in the wide areas. And if the defense blitzes, the Y and running backs become prime receivers.

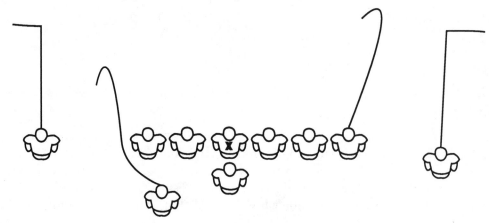

A mirrored pattern

Here are the rules and keys for this pass—greatly simplified. The full explanation of the rules would take seven long paragraphs.

Flanker (Z) looks at the near cornerback and safety. If the corner is 5 to 10 yards deep, it could be a man-to-man or a zone. If the safety is closer to the line of scrimmage than the corner, it is probably a zone. In any case, run a 10-yard out pattern (the basic pattern shown above). But if the cornerback is up close, he will probably try to bump and run (a tight man-to-man), or bump and play the short flat zone. In either case run a fade pattern (angling for a spot 18 yards deep and 4 yards from the sideline).

Split end (X) is similar to the flanker, but he must also look at the near linebacker for additional keys. His primary responsibilities are the same (run a 10 yard out or fade pattern if defenders are up close), but he may also get to the 10 yard out area (2 yards from the sideline) by splitting wider then hooking out at the 10 yard area.

The tight end (Y) looks first at the strong safety to determine whether he is in a zone or man coverage. On the snap of the ball he concentrates on the nearest linebacker. He tries to run an 8 yard hook over the middle, but if the linebacker won't let him inside he breaks to the outside. If the defense is blitzing he can break wherever there is an opening. If he gets man coverage from the free safety, he works upfield then comes back for the ball.

Running backs check to see if they are needed in pass protection, then release to an area 4 yards deep and between the offensive tackle and the wide receiver.

The quarterback looks at the secondary first. He will have called for the flanker side (80) or the split end side (60) to be the primary target area. So he will concentrate on that side first in his read. If the safeties are closer than normal (inverted), there is probably strong run support or man- for-man coverage. He should throw the out pattern to the wide receiver. If it is covered he should look at the back and tight end to see who is open. If the alignment shows that the wide outs are tightly covered, he should look at the defensive end or outside linebacker to the primary side to see if he has dropped off in pass coverage. If he hasn't, one of the backs or the tight end should be open.

Remember that this is just one of many patterns, each with its own set of reads. Each read is more complicated because the keys can cover three and four deep alignments, regular formations and inverted formations, tight and normal zones and man for man defenses, as well as situations in which the blitz occurs.

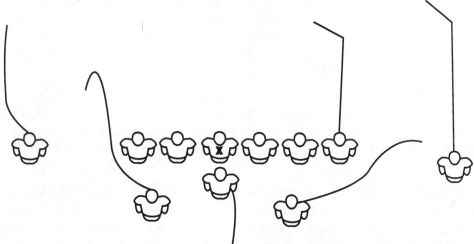

Options of alignment and patterns for the Purdue 60-80 pattern

Here is a BYU pattern in which the halfback is the primary receiver. The split end runs a fly pattern to clear the area and stretch the defense vertically. The tight end comes across the field working to a depth of 15 to 18 yards in the zone vacated by the defensive back who is covering the split end. The halfback runs into the short zone area to the same side. This is a type of flood pattern. Meanwhile the flanker is running a 20 yard in pattern which should be open if the defense is in a man to man cover. If the quarterback reads it as a zone defense, he looks first to the halfback, then the tight end, then the deep man—split end. If it is a man-to-man he can start with the same read, but can figure that the flanker will eventually get free.

The halfback, being the prime receiver, looks at the linebackers. If the two near linebackers drop for the pass, he should get about 6 yards into their territory and split them (get between them), then turn to catch the ball.

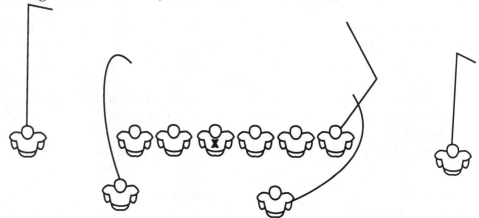

BYU pattern with halfback as primary receiver

Here is another pattern in which the halfback is the primary receiver. The wide receivers get into patterns at a 15 yard depth—in the seam between the backers and the deep defensive backs. The tight end gets deep to drive off the safeties and make certain that there is a seam for the wide receivers. The running backs get a depth of 5 yards into the secondary and get in the seams between the linebackers. This should work if the defense is a three deep zone.

Against a two deep zone, the wide receivers go wide and deep. With the tight end deep in the middle and the wide receivers deep on the sidelines, the QB can look at the two defensive backs and determine which of the three receivers is most likely to be open.

If the receiver reads that the defense is in man-to-man, the tight end runs a sharp post to get away from the strong safety, the wide receivers comeback patterns should help them to get free (but if the safety takes away the inside, the end runs an "out"), and the running backs run to the flats. Their speed should help to free them from the slower linebackers.

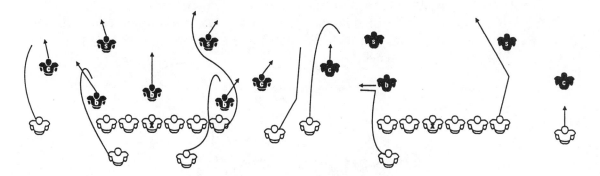

Pattern with halfback primary—vs three deep

Adjustment vs two deep safeties

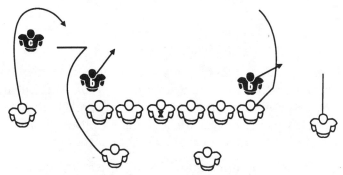

Adjustment vs man for man

Here is an all curl pattern which the Seahawks use. On the two receiver side it is probable that only one of the receivers will be double covered. Once the QB sees who the linebacker is covering, he can be reasonably certain that the other receiver can break free.

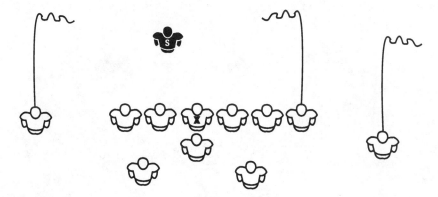

Seahawk all curl pattern

Here is a pattern which the Chargers have used which should work against a zone or a man defense. The inside curl pattern crosses the outside curl pattern. Versus a zone both receivers can look for the seams and versus a man defense the crossing gives the effect of a pick.

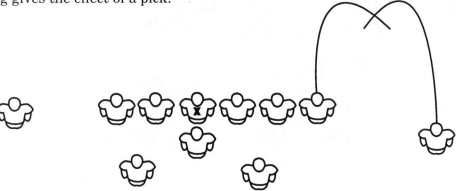

Chargers crossing curl

Each defensive alignment has obvious advantages and disadvantages. A team playing a tight bump and run, like the Raiders, loses some of the support for the run from the cornerbacks while they take away most of the short patterns. The Raiders will generally have only a single free safety to back up the whole field, but they hope that the speed and skill of their cornerbacks will give them the advantage they need.

Many teams playing bump and run will keep two safeties deep. College and high school teams are more likely to do this. Here is a pattern which Terry Donahue at U.C.L.A. uses against such defenses. He sends the wide receivers down deep to occupy the corners and safeties. Then he can work his other three receivers against the three linebackers. This usually works to his advantage.

U.C.L.A. also gives more freedom to receivers to get open in a specific area. The QB then just looks left to right or right to left to find the first open man—then fires.

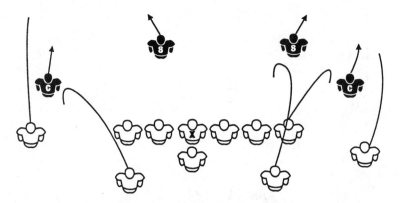

A U.C.L.A. pattern which works the seams across the field

The run and shoot offense of "Tiger" Ellison, and refined and popularized by "Mouse" Davis of Portland State and the Lions, originally offered five series—each with its own reads. It had reads in its running attack and reads in its passing plays.

Here is the tight double slot formation with the left half in motion. This is called the "gangster pass right" series. When this play was called in the huddle no one on the offense knew which of the options would develop.

1. If the man covering the left end was three or more yards inside the end the QB could throw the automatic pass. The X end would run an "arrow" pattern.

2. Where would the fourth defensive man from the center play after the left half went in motion? Was he close to the slotback (blitz position), head up on the split end (hardnose position), or halfway between and dropped off a bit (walkaway position)? If the number 4 defender was in a blitz position, the right end would run a look in pattern. The QB would run down the line and throw on his third step.

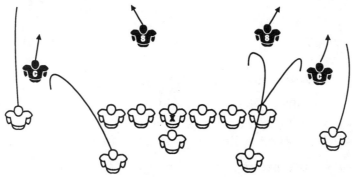

Against a blitz position number 4 man

Against the walkaway 4 man, the right end would start downfield, make a 30 degree break and curl. The slot would hook near the inside linebacker so that he could "cherry pick" him, and the motion man would swing wide. The rule was " He left—I right; he right—I left; he up—I back; he back—I up." In other words, if the walkaway number 4 man came up or went wide the pass would be thrown to the end running a curl. If the walkaway man dropped off or came to the middle, the QB would hit the halfback in motion.

The right halfback might also be the pass receiver. His rule was that if the near linebacker red dogged he would release upfield as a hot receiver and catch the ball over his inside shoulder. If the backer followed the motion man, the right slotback would release and catch the ball over his outside shoulder. If he played in his normal position, the slot would pick him by running a hook pattern between the linebacker and the curling end.

If a team consistently ran a hardnose cornerback on the split end, there was a special pass called. It was not part of the basic series of reads.

Another adjustment that often had to be made was controlling a defender who followed the motion man across the field. In this situation the QB would throwback to the left end, who would have single coverage, or the QB would call this special play. The ball was snapped early to allow the right slotback to pick the "unwelcomed stranger" as he covered man for man, worked to the flat zone, or dropped to the hook zone.

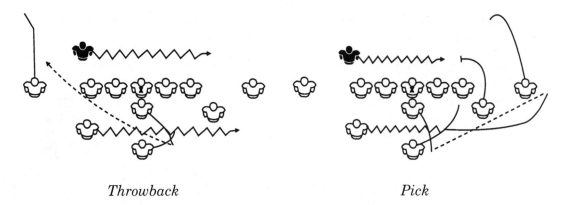

Throwback   *Pick*

Handling the "unwelcomed stranger"

This run and shoot offense was designed for a high school team, so you see that reading defenses can be done at any level of football. In fact, it must be done if the passing attack is to be worked to its maximal potential.

This reading and interpreting the defense is essential to any modern passing attack. It must be quick and it must be accurate. And it must be done with at least a half ton of charging maniacs intent on destroying your body. Still we expect quarterbacks to stay calm while being attacked by 280 pound monsters charging him with an intent to kill. They really do earn their money.

ATTACKING MAN TO MAN DEFENDERS

The simplest strategy would be to just outrun the defender who is playing man-to-man. But there are two possible problems. If you are playing at the pro level you are being bumped for 5 yards then you are going to have to outrun cornerbacks who run 4.4 for the 40. They are pretty quick. If you were playing a team which plays a looser man-to-man, as the Cowboys do, the defender has a head start of three to 10 yards on you. Consequently most man-to-man routes require that the receiver use techniques to break away from the defender. The simplest such moves are the hooks and the outs.

Hook   *Out*

In order to free himself, the receiver may lean into the defender to get him off balance, then make his break.

If the defender stays close to the receiver, a double breaking route such as a hook and go, an out and up, or an in and out (Z out) can be called—if the QB has time for these slower patterns.

Hook and go   *Out and up*

In and out

Another common route against bump and run cover is the fade route. In this route the receiver runs to the corner of the end zone fading away from the passer. The ball must be thrown over the defender while the receiver uses his body to keep the receiver away from the spot where the ball will be caught. A short pass is an easy interception, so the passer must hit it exactly—or overthrow it.

Pick plays, where one man screens another's defender, are a common pattern, especially on the goal line—where most teams play man coverage.

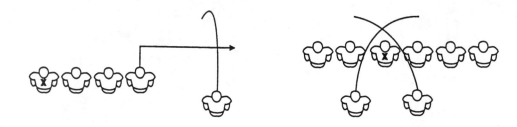

Two man pick   *Crossing backs pick*

COUNTERS FOR THE PASSING ATTACK

Just as running teams must have counters, so must passing teams. Teams that drop their linebackers quickly to stop the pass may be countered with the fullback or quarterback draws.

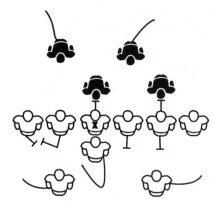

Fullback draw with a trap   *Quarterback draw*

Screen passes may work against teams that rush a good many players. While the receivers run deep and the quarterback drops nine or more steps, the linemen set up a screen for the receiver.

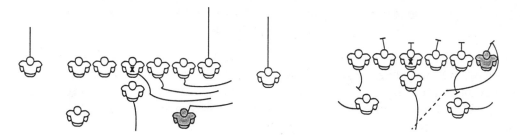

Halfback screen right   *Tight end middle screen*

The shovel pass was developed by Jack Curtice and popularized when Lee Grosscup played for him at Utah. It has had a resurgence among both college and pro teams lately. However, none of the teams using it have achieved the perfection of execution that Jack and Lee enjoyed.

In the Curtice shovel pass, one side of the line dropped back in a retreating pass protection. The other side blocked aggressively as if for a run. The receiver, usually a tight end or running back, would run to the gap created by the different blocking schemes and take a short pass, often an underhanded or a basketball chest pass. He would then run into the secondary where he would option the first man who tried to tackle him. The player to whom he would lateral would often score.

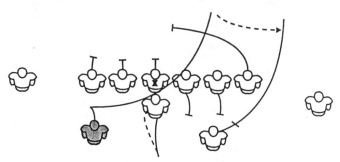

Jack Curtice's shovel pass

PASSING IS MORE THAN THROWING AND CATCHING

Don Shula, of the Dolphins, has described passing as a mental achievement, while throwing is strictly physical. He has said that his quarterback, Dan Marino, reads the defense and makes up his mind as to where he will throw faster than anyone who has ever played the game. Marino not only recognizes where to throw but how to throw—hard or soft, high and outside, or low and inside.

Obviously there is a lot of thought and teaching time which must go into developing a comprehensive passing attack. It is certainly the easiest way to move the ball, but it takes a great deal of time to teach proper throwing and catching techniques, how to run routes, how to protect the passer, and how to read the defenses. The pros have the time to develop this type of game. Some colleges take the time. And as Tiger Ellison has shown us, it is possible in high schools too.

There are some disadvantages of the passing attack. Cold and wet weather can make it much tougher to pass. And high school teams that don't platoon their offensive and defensive squads may not want to pass too much because passing games take longer. With the clock stopping after each incomplete pass there are more plays per game. A non-platooning team tires if they passed a lot.

Even so, it cannot be denied that a good passing attack can move the ball and can score more often. Tiger Ellison said that before he developed his run and shoot offense, his team scored about every 20 plays. With the run and gun attack they scored about every ten plays.

There is no question that modern football, just as modern warfare, is relying increasingly on the air force—and the BOMB.

9

A Look at the Defense

Most experienced coaches know that you win with defense. The different defensive alignments, the unexpected stunts and blitzes, and the varying coverages can make those previously mentioned running plays and blocking schemes very difficult to execute.

With equal material a team should be able to stop the 11 offensive players with 17 men. If the defense ran a gap eight alignment to stop the run and had defenders in all six short zones and in all of the deep three passing zones, the offense would be hard pressed to move the ball. Unhappily for defensive coordinators, the rules committee still only allows 11 men on each side of the ball. So the problem is how to get the maximum running and passing defense with only 11 men.

The offense has many advantages over the defense. It knows whether the play will be a run or a pass. It knows the point of attack, and it knows the snap count. In the old days the defenders' major advantage was that they were able to use their hands and arms much more than the offensive players. But with the new rules, the offensive blockers are allowed to extend their hands in blocking. This greatly reduces the defensive advantage.

Another change which hurts the pro defense is not being able to bump pass defenders once they have passed beyond 5 yards of the line of scrimmage. This really hurt Bump and Run pass coverage teams. (High school and college defenders are still allowed to bump offensive players as long as they are potential blockers.)

With the rules, especially the professional rules, favoring the offense, the defensive effectiveness is reduced. There is the desire of the defensive coordinators to hold the opponents scoreless. So there is great pressure on the defensive team. Defensive linemen must stop the run in their areas of responsibility and pursue the ball carrier if it is in another area. At the same time, they must be ready to rush the passer aggressively and still react to the draw play or the screen pass. The linebackers must stop the run, yet still react to their zones if a pass develops. Defensive backs must stop all the long and short pass patterns while still helping to make the tackle if a running play develops.

In order for a defensive team to stop an offensive team it must be in an effective alignment, use the proper keys to get the defenders to the right spot, and have techniques which will allow these duties to be accomplished.

DEFENSIVE ALIGNMENTS

Early defensive teams generally used the tight six man line, with the fullback and center as linebackers, and the other offensive backs as defensive backs in a three deep alignment. They played man-to-man pass defense with the defensive halfbacks on the offensive ends and the quarterback as a safety.

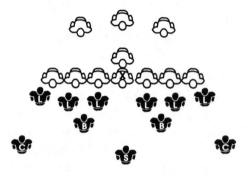

Tight 6

Soon the 5-3 and 7 diamond alignments came into being to stop the pass or the run more effectively and to confuse the blocking assignments. The linemen either crouched low and charged through the offensive linemen to their areas of responsibility or stood up and used their hands to ward off the offensive blockers.

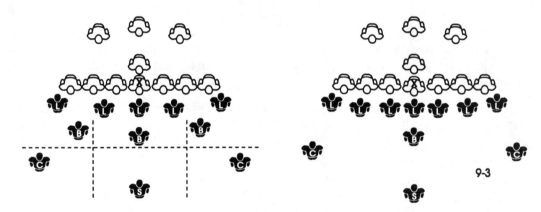

5-3 (with three short pass zones and three deep zones)

7 diamond

As offenses attacked more effectively, defenses were forced to become more effective in alignment and in technique. General Robert Neyland, the coach at Tennessee, developed the wide tackle 6 which reduced the offense's ability to run wide but it increased the vulnerability to run between the guards. So this weak area had to be strengthened by having outstanding athletes with effective techniques at the guard spots. Sam Boghosian, former Raider offensive line coach, and Dave Levy, longtime Charger and Detroit Lion assistant, played these positions side by side at U.C.L.A. on the 1954 national championship team. What they lacked in size they made up for in technique and toughness.

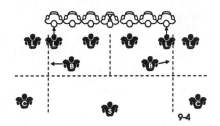

Wide tackle 6 (ends and backers could drop into four short zones, while defensive backs covered the three deep zones)

As pursuit to the ball became more a necessity, linebackers were moved closer to the middle so that they could pursue both sides of the field more effectively. Then the ends were dropped back to become outside linebackers.

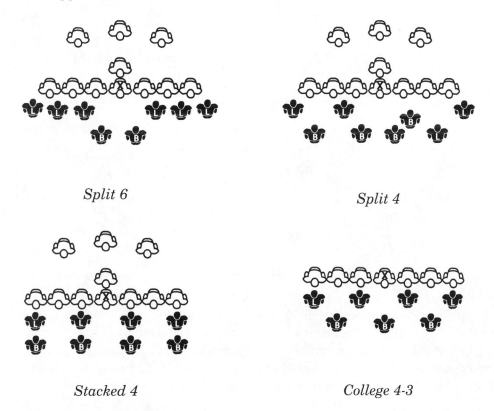

Split 6   Split 4

Stacked 4   College 4-3

As the passing game with wide receivers developed in the pros and as the split-T option attack took over with the colleges, coaches began to work with four defensive backs.

Steve Owens of the New York Giants is credited with being the first to use the umbrella defense with four defensive backs. In his 6-1 umbrella the ends and linebacker could drop to the three hook areas while the cornerbacks could cover the flats (a 5 under, 2 deep zone), or one back could rotate to the flat with the others playing three deep (a 4 under, 3 deep zone). With a run to one side, the defensive backs could rotate up and still be in a 3 deep secondary.

Here is the seven man front with four defensive backs.

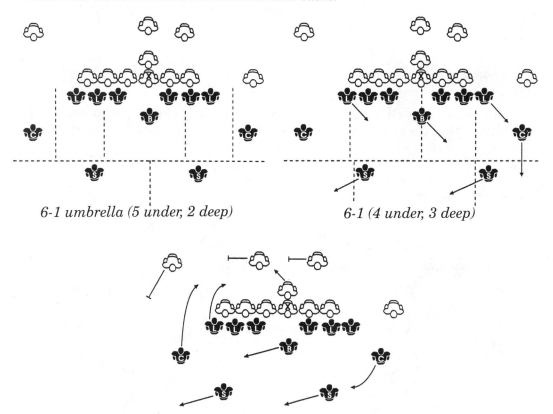

6-1 umbrella (5 under, 2 deep)   *6-1 (4 under, 3 deep)*

6-1 with umbrella rotating to a wide run or run-pass option

Using four defensive backs made it easier to vary the coverage, changing the zones which each defender covered, and to play man to man pass defense. It also made it easier to adjust the defense to the offensive strength. If a team came out in a winged formation all that an umbrella defense had to do was rotate with a cornerback becoming a defensive end. An eight man front team would have to adjust linemen and/or backers to meet the offensive strength.

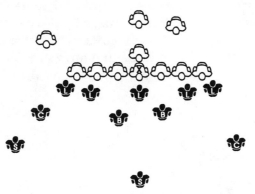

Okie, or 3-4, with a rotated secondary to adjust to a wing T

With the soundness of the four deep backs proven, Earle "Greasy" Neale of the Philadelphia Eagles developed a new alignment, now called the Eagle. He used a middle guard who was tough enough to stop up the inside, yet could pursue. His tackles took the guard-tackle gap, often crashing down to stop the trap play. The tackle who was on the pulling guard might stop the play from behind, while the tackle who was being trapped would be playing the trap block aggressively. The ends could crash down to stop the off tackle play. The linebackers played on the ends, so they had a good tip as to whether the play was a run at them or a pass or run to the opposite side. (If the end released, it was a pass or a run the other way.)

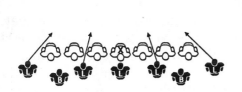

Eagle defense

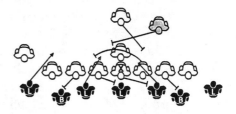

Eagle versus the inside trap

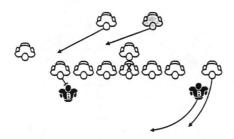

End releasing (indicating pass or run opposite)

This became the forerunner of the modern pro 4-3 defense. The thinking was that if you wanted the tackles to crash to the guards, why not put them there to start. If you wanted the ends to get to the off tackle area, why not align them there. If the middle guard (often called "Mike" for middle-in man) was to pursue the play why not move him back to a linebacker spot (where he was often called "Mac" meaning middle back).

Eagle   *Pro 4-3*

Meanwhile, in the late 1940s and the early 1950s with the split-T attacks becoming more potent and more generally used in college, it was found that the normal eight man front was ineffective in stopping it. So Bud Wilkinson of Oklahoma developed the defense to stop it. The Okie 5-2 is still the most common defense in high school and college and is the father of the pro 3-4 defense.

In the Okie defense, the nose guard had to be able to control both sides of the offensive center and stop the quarterback sneak. The tackles had to control the outside of the offensive tackle for the dive play. The linebackers keyed the guards and mirrored their movements in order to react to the pass, the inside dive, or the trap. The ends had to stop the off tackle play and the quarterback on the option. The cornerbacks played closer to the line than they did in Steve Owens' umbrella. They would rotate up if the flow of the backs came towards them. Their job would be to take the widest back—the man to whom the quarterback might pitch. The other backs had now rotated into a three deep.

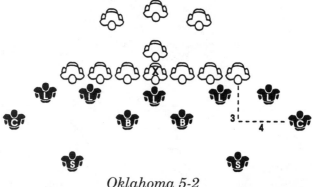

Oklahoma 5-2

Reactions of the linebackers to the keys of the offensive guards.

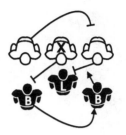

Guards block straight (a dive or wide play)

One guard blocks down, one pulls—trap play

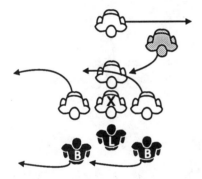

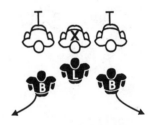

Guards pull in a counter

Guards pass block

TECHNIQUES OF LINEPLAY

Some coaches believe in constantly attacking the offense with their defense. In this scheme, the defensive linemen will either charge through an offensive lineman or through a gap in the line. Stunting teams use this technique with their linemen and their linebackers.

A slant charge is used to go from a man to a gap or from a gap into a man. It changes the attacking point one half man. A loop is used to go from one man to another or to a gap. It moves the attacking point at least one man away from where the defender originally line up.

Here are some examples of stunts using line slants and loops with blitzing backers.

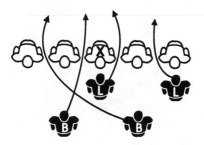

Middle guard-backer stunt (from a 5-3 alignment)

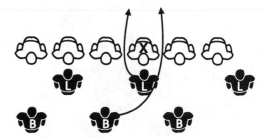

Tackles in a twist move

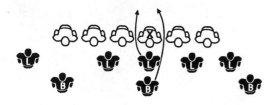

Seahawk stunt

Noseguard-linebacker stunt

A team may align in one defense then all slant or loop to one side or the other. They might be instructed to slant to the strong side of the formation or to the wide side of the field.

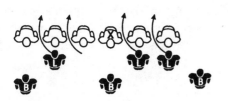

Slant to tight end

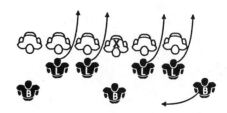

Slant away from tight end

Buddy Ryan's 46 defense at Chicago was an attacking type of defense. It had so many people near the ball that it forced the offense to make a number of adjustments when designing a running play or pass protection against it. Of course, there were a couple of pretty fair football players which made it go!

The advantages of the penetrating defenses are that if the defenders guess right, they are at the point of attack and can drop the runner for a loss. Also, if a pass develops, the defensive linemen are already in their pass rush and gain a few steps over where they would be if they were reading the defensive lineman. The disadvantages are that if the play goes away from the lineman, he is not in a good position from which he can pursue the play, so it might break for a long gain.

Many teams will only penetrate on stunts, which they call very seldom. Their main concern is that the offense doesn't get the easy score. They use techniques in which the defender reads one or more linemen then reacts to the ball, generally not crossing the line of scrimmage. It is hoped that if all the defenders react correctly, the offensive team can't make more than two yards per running play. They will then have to punt on fourth down and four yards to go.

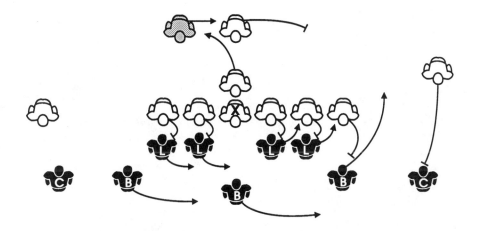

A pro 4-3 defense reading and reacting to the flow

The simplest read is to read the offensive blocker's head. If he puts his head on your right side it is obvious that he is trying to block you away from the play, which must be going to your right. So by using a forearm rip or a hand shiver the defender should be able to free himself from the blocker, move across his face then make the tackle. In this technique it is essential that the defender not go behind the blocker, or he will not be able to pursue quickly.

Block to defender's right   *Pass block*

A more complicated read is that which the nose guard (called a nose tackle in the pros) must make. He must be able to read the one-on-one block, the trap block, and the pass block and must be able to handle the double team block.

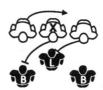

One-on-one   *Angle blocking*

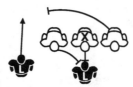

Double team and trap on tackle

DEFENSIVE LINE THEORY

Some coaches want the defender to control the man in front of him. If he can do this, he will be able to control the gaps on each side of him. This is what was expected of the guards in the previously mentioned wide tackle 6. With the skill and the size of today's offensive linemen, it is often difficult to totally control a man and both gaps. Consequently many coaches have changed their defensive theory to that of gap control. In a gap control defense the defender may still play on an offensive lineman, but he has primary responsibility for only one of the gaps.

Some coaches just call a defense: okie, eagle, split 4, or the 5-3, for example. The defenders know just where to line up for each defense. To upset the offense the team might overshift or undershift its line. When doing this the linebackers would generally shift the other way so that the defense is still balanced.

3-4 overshifted to tight end side

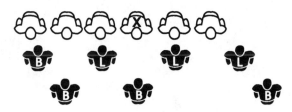

An undershifted 3-4

At Alabama some years ago, Bear Bryant popularized the numbers defense. This allowed for a great deal of variation in calling defenses. By calling a number the player knew where to line up and what technique to play. The system has become so common that today when most coaches talk to each other about defensive line play they talk about "the 1 technique" or "the 5 technique."

The 0, 4, and 6 techniques were head up reading techniques by the nose guard, tackle and end. The 1 and 7 techniques were inside gap control techniques used by the defensive tackle and end, and the 3 and 9 techniques were outside gap control techniques used by the tackle and end. When the linebacker called two appropriate numbers, he could align the linemen on his side of the ball in many different spots. The linebacker would then go to the appropriate spot. For example, if the linebacker on the tight end side called a 59, his side of the line would be an Okie 5-2 and if the weakside linebacker called a 03, his side of the line would be an "Eagle."

LINEBACKER PLAY

As we mentioned at the beginning of this chapter, a good defense would have at least 17 men on the field—eight linemen and nine pass defenders. Since we are only allowed eleven men, some must do double duty. The linebackers are the primary double duty players. They must stop the running play, and they must defend against the pass. Many plays are designed to force the linebacker into mistakes. The play action pass, for example, makes the linebacker play run while a receiver sneaks into the pass zone which he should be covering. The draw play coaxes the linebacker to drop back, then a run comes at him. The counter type of play gets him moving one direction then attacks in the other direction.

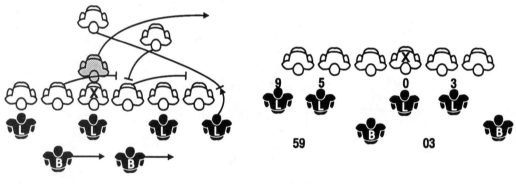

Play action pass   *Draw play*

The keys which the backers use to react to run or pass are varied. An outside backer playing on an end may just key his end. If the end releases, the backer drops. Of course, he will need an additional key to make certain that the area which he is vacating will not be attacked by a running play, especially a counter action or a reverse.

Inside backers may key the uncovered lineman. As was mentioned in the Okie 5-2 the backer can mirror the guards and, if the guards drop back in pass protection on every pass and there are no play action passes, the linebacker should be able to handle both run and pass responsibilities.

Another way that linebackers can cover two areas of responsibility is in controlled stunting. If the running keys are valid, one linebacker may be asked to scrape into a gap in the line and react as a slanting lineman. The other backer would then be asked to shuffle to back up the area vacated by the scraping backer.

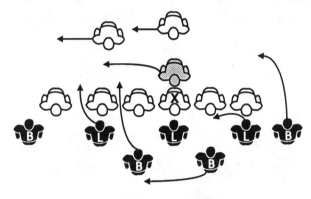

Flow left

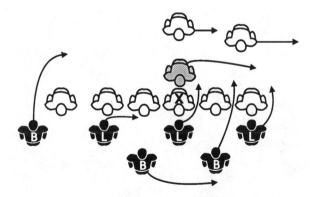

Flow right (backers scrape and shuffle)

With the defensive linemen shooting the other gaps, the defense gets the same effect as a gap 8 goal line defense, yet only five men were committed to the charge.

In order to get the linebackers to react correctly their keys must be nearly fool-proof. Here are some examples of keys (looking at only one player) and reads (looking at two or more players).

If the attack of the offense doesn't cross its back, a key of the near back is the easiest. In the traditional split T attack there was no crossing action so a straight key was possible. However, because the counter came from the fullback, the offside linebacker would have to first key his halfback, stop the dive threat, then check the fullback for the counter.

Here is an example of an Okie defense (tackle with outside responsibility) stunting to an Eagle (tackle has inside responsibility). The scraping linebacker leaves his responsibility over the guard and takes the area inside the offensive end. The shuffling linebacker changes his key from the near halfback to the fullback after the first step.

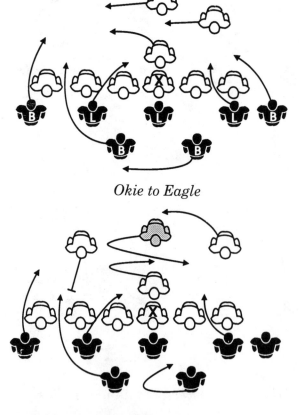

Okie to Eagle

Split T series right (shuffle backer takes fullback counter)

When a team uses series in which the backs cross, such as in many trapping series or cross bucks, the key for that game must be the offside back. By keying him the backer is right whether or not the backs cross.

Crossbuck with backers   Split T series — scraping and shuffling

If teams pull their guards in countering actions, such as reverses, the backers will have to read through the guards to the backs. Depending on whether the backs cross or not, the backer's read could be near guard to near back or near guard to far back. If the guard pulls, he becomes the main key; if not, the back is the key.

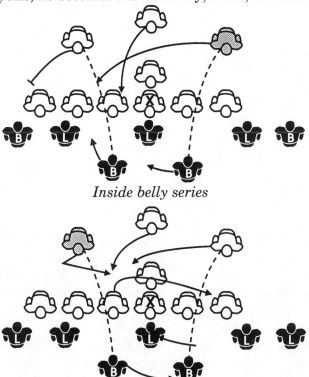

Inside belly series

Belly counter with guard pulling (straight read through the guard)

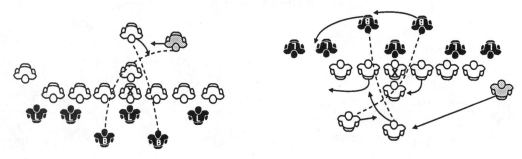

Crossbuck from wing T

Crossbuck reverse
(cross read – guard to far back)

As the level of football becomes more complex, the reads may be expanded. Often they include three players in a triangle. For example, the inside linebacker might have to read the guard, tackle, and the near back. If the linemen block straight ahead, the back becomes the key. If one or both linemen pull, they are usually the better key.

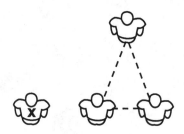

Triangle for inside backer

If the offensive coordinator is aware of the keys being used, he may use a play or a blocking scheme which will take advantage of the key. If the pull of the guard is one of the keys, the offense can install an "influence trap." In this play one guard pulls wide and the other guard pulls across the center to block the backer or tackle who is being influenced outward by the wide pull. A draw play is another type of key breaker. If the backers are keying the offensive backs only, a bootleg will break the key. On the goal line, where most teams play man to man defense, the quarterback seldom has a man assigned to him. Consequently the naked bootleg (no leading blockers) often works for a score.

TECHNIQUES OF THE DEFENSIVE BACKS

The defensive back's technique depends on whether he is playing a man to man or a zone. Generally, the back will take a few steps back as he takes his key. A defensive halfback may key the offside end or end and tackle. If both go downfield (in a college or high school game), it is a run or pass behind the line. (In high school and college the linemen can go downfield on passes completed behind the line of scrimmage.) Of course in a pro game, the tackle going downfield can only indicate a run.

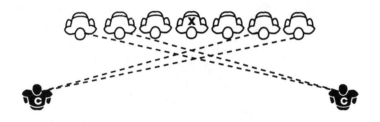

Keying the off tackle and end

The defensive back might also key any uncovered linemen, such as the guards in an Okie alignment. But with so many teams pulling their uncovered linemen behind the line of scrimmage, they have taken away this key for many of the plays.

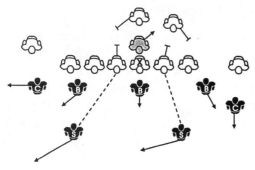

Uncovered guards drop for pass blocking   *Guards go after backers*

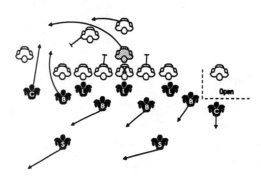

Keying uncovered linemen

Zone teams will drop to their zones if a pass shows. They may also rotate their zones if the passer moves to a new position.

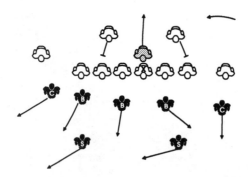

Backs and backers dropping to their zones (4 under, 3 deep)

Backs and backers react to a rollout pass by changing their responsibilities. Note that because the player in the strongside flat comes up to force the play and the others have rotated, there is no one in the flat zone away from the flow. While the throwback pass to that area is usually open, it is very hard to complete.

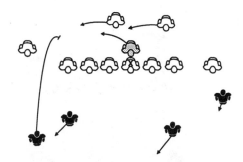

Rollout with corner forcing the pass

With teams passing more, especially in certain situations, defensive coaches have begun to put in more defensive backs than the standard four. The five back (nickel defense) and the six back (dime defense) have defensive backs coming in to substitute for linebackers on passing downs. The advantage of such moves is that the backs have better speed and pass defense skills—and are less likely to be burned in man-to-man coverage against running backs. The disadvantage is that they tend to be weaker against the run than the linebackers would have been.

THEORY OF SECONDARY ALIGNMENT

It takes three men to cover the deep secondary. Consequently many teams use the three deep secondary which has been around since the dawn of the game. Others will rotate or otherwise disguise their intentions as to who will be in each zone.

Originally the four deep backs were in an umbrella alignment. This made it easy to rotate to the flow of the backs.

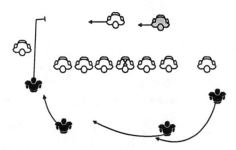

Umbrella—rotating to flow

With more teams using two wide receivers, it became impossible to rotate up to stop the run because it would leave the wide receiver unattended. So many teams started to invert their safeties. The safeties then became responsible for the run support while the corners were primarily responsible for the pass.

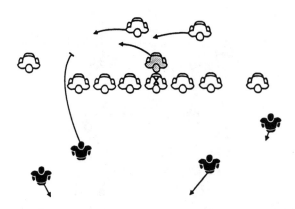

Inverted 4 deep with safeties supporting to the flow

With the umbrella defense or the invert, when teams played a zone defense they generally played with three deep backs in the zones. Some college and high school coaches decided that they could teach better if they had the same three people in the deep zones all the time, but they liked the seven man front of the Okie defense. So with seven up front and three deep they had an extra man. He was called the rover back. Frank Broyles at Arkansas termed him "the monster," a name that became almost universal for teams using the rover.

The rover or monster could be put in the middle of the defense, but usually he went to the wide side of the field or to the strength of the offensive set. In determining the strength of the offense, his rules were to go to the side of a flanker or slot back or away from a split end. This rover back usually had responsibility for wide runs and for the wide flat pass zone.

In man-to-man defense the defenders can play up close and bump and run with the receiver. College and high school defensive backs can continue to bump the receiver until the pass is thrown. At the pro level, in order to increase the scoring and appeal more to the fans, the bump was limited to just one per play.

While there is usually a free safety, he cannot cover the whole deep secondary. The cornerbacks must do most of the job themselves. If the receiver is faster than the defender, he can easily get open on a streak pattern. Teams running the bump and run have the theoretical advantage of being able to take away all of the patterns that the receiver might run. The major disadvantage is that the man covering a wide receiver can't be much help in stopping the running play.

Many teams play man to man defense while backed off 5 to 10 yards from the receiver. This has the advantage of being able to take away the long pass with a slower defender and possibly getting some run support from the cornerback. But it has the disadvantage of being open to underneath patterns and to double cutting patterns such as the out and up or hook and go.

SELECTING THE TYPE OF DEFENSE

Since there are so many possible alignments of the line and backers and there are several common types of pass coverage, the coach must determine which alignments and coverages he will use. This will be based on his own preference, such as four rather than three linebackers, or a zone defense rather than man-to-man. He must determine whether he wants to hit and pursue with his linemen or to attack through the offense and hope for the big play.

Some coaches like to use multiple defensive fronts hoping to upset the blocking rules of the offense. Other coaches prefer to sit in one defense and have the players master the techniques necessary for that one alignment.

In the defensive secondary, some coaches will opt for one primary defense. Others will vary their defenses. At the high school level, if the teams in the league run a great deal, the coach may decide on one defensive coverage. But if a team is going to face sophisticated passing attacks, whether at the high school or pro level, more than one coverage will definitely be selected. When you give a quarterback only one kind of defensive look, he should be able to pick apart the defense—because every defense will have at least two major holes in the zones being covered.

It therefore becomes essential for a defense to be able to give different "looks" during the game. Some coaches want to put their players in the best position to play the defense. For example, if they are in man-to-man, they may bring the corners up to the receivers. But if they are in zone they may drop off 7 to 10 yards. This gives the quarterback a good pre-snap read of the defense. Other coaches prefer to keep their players in the same pre-snap positions then move to their responsibilities after the snap of the ball. They may lose a little in their ability to play the perfect defense, but they take away the early reads of the quarterback and make him play less than perfect offense.

As you watch the game, see if you can pick out the possible cheats by the defensive backs then figure out what they will do from their pre-snap alignment. You can bet that the quarterback and the coaches in the press box are watching for these tip-offs.

Carlton Gray

10

THE KICKING GAME
AND SPECIAL TEAMS

George Allen is credited with hiring the first special teams coach. Lots of coaches talked about the importance of the kicking game, but sly old George was the one who put his money were his mouth was.

Today as there is such an emphasis on special teams, the kicking game has become more important in the eyes of the fans. Coaches, especially the field position coaches, have long known this and have emphasized the kicking game in practice and in the game. A number of coaches believe that if a team makes two more mistakes in the kicking game than its opponents, it will almost undoubtedly lose that game. A blocked punt, a long kick return, or a missed extra point can be disastrous to a team's chance of winning.

To emphasize the importance of the kicking aspects of the game, many college head coaches have taken over the kicking game as their part of the practice. This emphasizes to the players how important this aspect of the game is. Many coaches have their team practice kicking first every afternoon.

Many of the so called breaks in a football game occur during the kicking phase of the game. They are not really breaks at all because the so-called lucky team has practiced all season to make those breaks occur.

The kicking game incorporates both offensive and defensive aspects. The punt and kickoff are defensive, but the kick returns, the field goal and extra points, the fake kicks, the punt and extra point blocks, and even the seldom seen quick-kick are thought of as offensive weapons.

THE KICKOFF

Most teams prefer to receive the kickoff if they win the coin flip, but strong defensive and kicking teams will often choose to kick the ball. Their hope is that they can hold their opponents inside the opponent's 30, make them punt, then take over somewhere around their own 40 yard line.

The basic kickoff play puts the kicker in the middle of the field with five tacklers on either side. Many coaches will use other alignments to increase the effectiveness of the play.

Some teams will put their kicker on the hashmark in order to reduce the opponent's options for a return. At the high school level this can give a real advantage. At the college level, because the hash marks are moved in, the advantage is lessened. At the pro level, where the hash marks are nearly in the center of the field, there is no real advantage to this type of kickoff.

Coaches who use the offset kickoff alignment believe that it will be more difficult for a team to return to the other side of the field. Every step that the ball carrier takes to the far sideline gives every member of the kicking team one more step into the receiver's territory, so their chances of an effective return are reduced. In addition, if the receivers return to the side of the kick, the defenders each have less territory to defend.

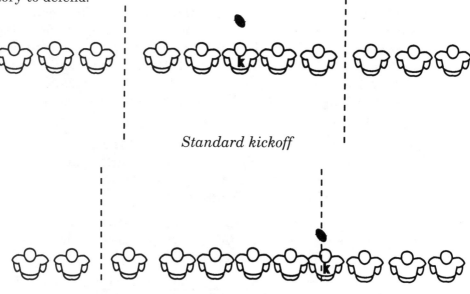

Standard kickoff

Offset kickoff alignment

Some coaches will start a couple of rushers farther back than the kicker so that they can get a longer and faster rush toward the receivers. Usually one of these men is a wedge breaker whose assignment is to dent the four or five man wedge of blockers which most teams use for their returns.

Some coaches will use two kickers, aligning one to kick to one side of the field with the other kicker ready to kick to the opposite field or to kick an onsides kick. In the following diagram, kicker 1 is used to kick deep to the right side of the field or to kick a dribbling straight ahead onside kick. Kicker 2 is used to kick shallower to the left or to kick the onsides kick across the field.

Such an array of kicks makes it much more difficult for the kick return team to prepare for an effective return since they must prepare to field two different types of onside kicks and kicks to the deep right and to the shallow middle off the field.

With all the soccer style kickers around today, there are many who can kick the ball into the end zone consistently. It doesn't take a genius to realize that this is the ultimate in kickoff strategy. The problem for the coach is when he doesn't have that great long ball kicker. One solution is to squib kick the ball.

To squib kick the ball, the kicker will generally lie the ball on its side rather than tee it up. He will also generally kick it off center so that it will take those uncontrolled bounces that only a football can take. So watching the receivers attempt to catch a squib kick is like watching Elmer Fudd trying to catch Bugs Bunny.

As you can see, there is a lot that can go into the thinking of a coach even for such a standard play as a kickoff. Covering the kickoff is another important consideration. Every kick coverage will have two men responsible for the outside. They are the ends. There will also be one or two men who act as safeties. The other seven or eight men will attack the ball carrier in one or two waves, keeping appropriate distances between themselves so that the ball carrier cannot easily go around them or run through a gap in the wave.

Most teams will have a couple of mad dogs who will sacrifice their bodies as they attempt to break the wedge of blockers who convoys the ball carrier until he finds a gap in the defense and runs for daylight.

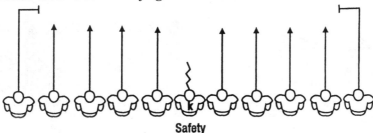

Safety

Straight kickoff coverage

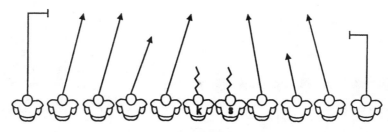

Safeties

Coverage with two waves

Because some teams assign men to block on the return many coaches will cross their rushers as they run downfield. This is particularly true of the ends, because many teams will use a trap on the end as part of their blocking scheme. So crossing the end and one or two other men can foul up the assignments of the return team.

Examples of crossing actions in kickoff coverage

THE KICKOFF RETURN

Generally the kickoff can be considered a success for the kickers if they hold the return team inside their own 25-yard line. It is a definite success for the returners if they get the ball to their own 35.

Kickoff return strategies involve either a wedge block, cross blocking, double teaming, trapping, or the setting up of a wall of blockers to one side of the field. These may also be used in combination.

A double wedge return

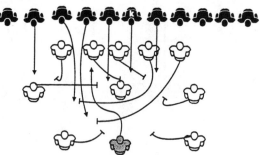

A cross block return

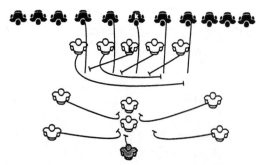

Cross block and wedge

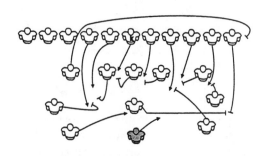

A trap on the end

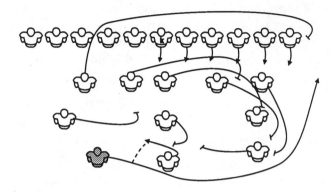

Reverse with a wall

The kickoff play gives coaches the opportunity for special trick plays. There is the reverse or fake reverse or the long lateral pass after the play starts one way the ball is suddenly on the other side of the field. Then there is the treacherous bubble play, in which the receiving team huddles around the ball before the kickers have a chance to get downfield. At the signal, all the receivers break their huddle, faking that they have the ball. The tackling team now has to sort out the real ball carrier and tackle him. It may not be the most effective play in football, but it sure is fun to practice. It was more effective when it was invented 80 years ago. The first bubble play coach had leather ovals, which simulated a football, sewn on each jersey. You can imagine the confusion among the tacklers — and we thought that the CIA was tricky!

THE PUNT

Many coaches believe that the punt is their most effective offensive play. How many plays average 35 to 40 yards?

In designing the punt play the coach must be concerned with the protection of the punter and with the coverage of the kick. The best protection is very tight, which reduces the effective coverage and the best coverage would place the kicking team members far apart, which would reduce the protection of the punter. A happy medium has to be achieved.

In high school and college, the kicking team members can release to cover the kick at any time. At the pro level only the widest two players can release immediately. The others have to wait until the ball has been kicked.

The long used tight punt formation gives good protection but is poor on coverage. It is often used today when a team is punting from its own end zone—and must avoid a blocked kick. In this formation the punter is generally ten yards behind the center.

In the traditional spread punt, the kicker lines up 13 to 15 yards behind the center. The halfbacks are in the center-guard gaps and the fullback lines up five to seven yards deep as a personal protector for the punter. This gives the effect of a nine man line. Some teams have actually used eight, nine or 10 man lines in their punt formations.

Another type of formation is the semi-spread or the tackles back formation. In this alignment the team has the advantage of seven men releasing quickly to cover yet having three big linemen as protectors for the punter.

In any of these formations the coach may elect to put one or two men extra wide. The Seahawks use both the spread punt and the spread punt with the ends wide.

An effective punting team will generally take less than 6/10 of a second to get the snap to the punter, then 1.2 or fewer seconds for the punter to get the kickoff. If the time from the snap to the kick is 1.8 or fewer seconds, it will probably not be blocked. If the time is 2.1 or more, there is a good chance of a blocked punt.

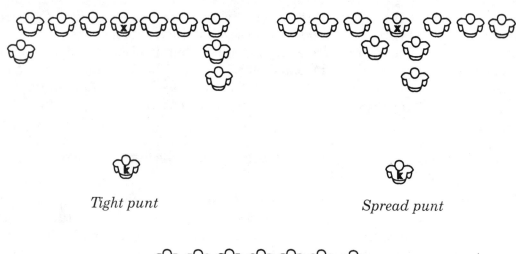

Tight punt   *Spread punt*

Semi-spread punt

Punt coverage usually starts with one or two men getting to the ball immediately. A second wave–generally the center, guards and tackles–will be 5 or 10 yards behind the first men. There will be two people designated to be ends or contain men who can stop any wide plays or reverses. Then there will be a safety man or two.

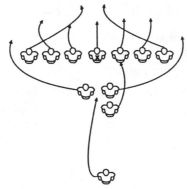

2-5-2-1-1

Since the object of the punt is to gain as many yards as possible, it is generally not best to kick into the end zone. The pros now keep statistics on how effective their punters are in starting their opponents inside their 20-yard line.

To kill the ball inside the 20, kickers will either kick out of bounds or use a squib punt, in which the ball is kicked to about the 10 while the covering team attempts to let the ball bounce toward the goal line but not cross it.

THE PUNT RETURN

The team defending a punt has the options of trying to block the punt or attempting to return it. Since it is so difficult to block a punt and it is so easy to rough the punter and give the punting team fifteen yards and a first down, most teams will opt to return the punt.

A team attempting to return the punt will generally try to hold up the tacklers on the punting team. With the pros being able to release only the two widest men on the snap of the ball, most teams will use two men to hold them up. At the high school and college level all potential tacklers should be delayed.

If the kicker can kick the ball high and get a good hang time the tacklers have more chance to cover the punt. Since it takes about two seconds for a kicker to get off his punt, and most good punters hang the ball up for about four seconds and kick about 35 to 40 yards, the punt coverage team has about six seconds to cover 35 to 40 yards. As most special teams players run a 40-yard dash in under five seconds, there is no chance for a return unless the coverage people are held up for at least two seconds.

Once the punting team members have escaped the men who were delaying them, the receiving team members set up for their return. Most teams will set up a wall on one side of the field. They generally choose the wide side of the field or a return left—against a right footed kicker. (The ball generally will drift to the right of a right footed kicker and to the left of a left footed kicker.)

The returning team obviously has to know whether they are going to block or return and to which side they will return. A few years ago in a major Southeast Conference game there was some confusion. When the ball was snapped the right side of the defense peeled off to the right, the left side peeled off to the left, and nobody rushed the punter. He alertly tucked the ball away and ran right up the middle for a fifty yard touchdown. Only the safety man realized that the ball hadn't been kicked!

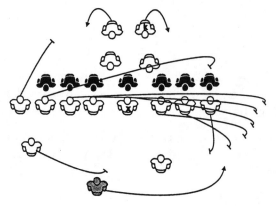

A sideline return with a single safety

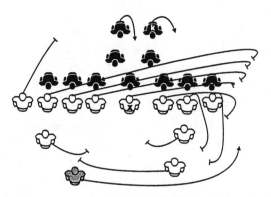

A sideline return with a reverse or a fake reverse

In the crisscross return, safety 1 knows that he will get the ball. If he catches the punt he will fake the reverse. If safety2 catches the punt he will hand to safety one.

The punt can be considered a success for the punting team if they net 35 yards. It is a success for the returners if the punt nets less than 25 yards.

PUNT BLOCKING

Often the scouting report will play a large part in determining whether or not to attempt to block the punt. A center who makes slow passes or who is often inaccurate may issue an invitation to block his team's punt. A kicker who takes too long to get off a punt or who takes more than two steps before kicking is a prime target for a block. Of course, there are tactical situations in which a block may be called, such as when behind late in the game or when the opponent is backed up close to his end zone.

Since the ball is generally kicked from about 3 yards in front of where the kicker started, most punt blockers are told to aim for a spot 4 to 5 yards in front of the kicker's starting point. This is about 8 or 9 yards behind the center. So the blockers have about 1.8 seconds to run 8 to 12 yards— depending on whether they are in the middle or the end of the defensive line.

Here is an example of a heavy rush in which there are six punt blockers against six blockers (excluding the offensive center who cannot be counted on to make the long snap then block effectively.) If any of the blockers choose the wrong man to block, a blocked punt may result.

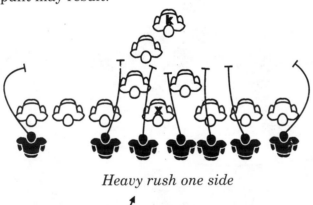

Heavy rush one side

Middle rush

A ten man rush (first used by the Philadelphia Eagles)

Every team will have at least one man rushing, just in case there is a bad snap. Some teams try to block every punt. Here is an example of a punt block which tries to spring three people free with the other eight in a return.

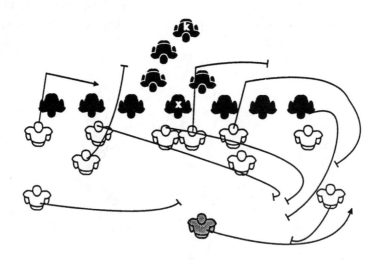

Double tandem rush and return

THE QUICK KICK

The field position advocates are strong advocates of the quick kick. They might use it on any down. Possession coaches seldom use a quick kick, and if they do, they are likely to use it only on third down and long yardage.

When properly executed, a quick kick can gain 60 or more yards, while a regular punt is more likely to gain only about 35. There is also little chance of a runback with a quick kick, and as many advocates of the quick kick have observed, there is a very high likelihood of a team clipping one of the members of the kicking team. So this adds another 15-yards to the kick.

FIELD GOALS AND EXTRA POINTS

There is no question that the abilities of the modern kickers have increased the chances of success of a field goal or extra point. Less than thirty years ago there were fewer than 100 field goals each year in major college football. Today there are hundreds each year.

Experience has found that it is best to tee up the ball about 7 to 8 yards behingd the center. The blockers then can block solid and force the defense around the kicking formation. If the kick is made within 1.2 seconds after the ball is snapped, it will probably be successful.

On field goals which are short the defending team has an opportunity to return the kick, so the kicking team must be alert to covering the ball after it is kicked.

Every team has at least one fake field goal as well as a special play which can be signalled if there is a foul up on the snap or the hold.

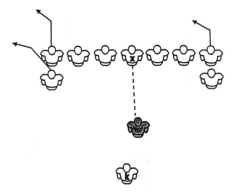

Emergency play—bad snap, holder yells "go," ends release for pass

DEFENDING THE FIELD GOAL

The defense must nearly always be ready for a fake field goal or extra point. The only exception would be for an extra point in a pro game where there is no opportunity to go for the two point conversion.

Most teams will try to block the field goal or extra point by either attempting to collapse the middle of the offensive line or by overloading at the end of the line. The scouting report will be very useful in determining the most obvious weakness in the offensive blockers.

MAKING THE BREAKS

As you can see, there are many opportunities for a big play when a team kicks. A blocked punt is at least a 50 yard gain for the blocking team (35 yards that would have been gained on the punt and the 15 yards behind the line where the kick was blocked).

11

STRATEGY—ADJUSTING TO NEXT WEEK'S OPPONENT

Since each football team will use the same offensive and defensive theories throughout the year opponents have a pretty good idea of what to expect in terms of formations, basic plays, and basic defensive alignments. The only team that did not fit this pattern was one of the Cal Tech teams of the late 1950s. The coach said that while they couldn't "out-physical" anybody they would have to try to "out-mental" their opponents. So every week the coach gave his players an entirely new offense. While they could master the new offense, they still couldn't master their opponents. Their record was 0-9 that year.

Scouting an opponent by attending a game or watching game films is standard at all levels of football. The formations, hash mark tendencies, position on the field tendencies, strongest and weakest players are all a part of the evaluation.

Some high schools may scout a team only once, but most big time colleges and the pro teams scout many games. The Seahawks generally scout an opponent's three last games plus their last few games against the Seahawks. This gives the coaches some insight into their basic theories and strategies, as well as a pretty good idea of which players will be playing against them.

Some high schools, most colleges, and all professional teams then take their scouting data and enter it into a computer. The computer can then quickly give a great deal of data on the upcoming opponent.

Percentages play a big part in developing the week to week strategy for an opponent. Do they have certain tendencies on third-and-one when the game is tied? Do those tendencies change if they are ahead or behind?

When Al Davis was the Raiders coach, most of the teams blitzed. So the Raiders worked a great deal on the types of blitzes that they expected to play against and how they could beat them. In those days, the players not only called the audibles, but also their own plays. The Raiders had special plays for certain blitzes, especially those that were difficult to disguise— such as a safety coming up into the line before the snap.

If a player could recognize a certain blitz before the snap, he might be able to call a special play to capitalize on the weakness of that defense. However, as a team might only run a certain blitz once or twice during a game, players had to make certain that they could recognize special blitzes the instant they were evident.

In the 1963 Raider game against the Oilers, the score was 35 to 35 at halftime. In the second half, one of the players recognized a special nine man blitz and called an audible with the fullback going in motion then turning upfield. Because the wide receivers were covered by the cornerbacks, only the defensive end was available to cover the fullback—who caught a pass good for 70 yards and a touchdown. This was probably the deciding score in their 52 to 49 victory.

Once the tendencies of the defense have been charted, the coach can begin to plan his own strategy of attack. If the opponent has shown marked tendencies against every opponent, it gives the coach a good hint as to what will work against the opponent.

Does the team nearly always stunt in a third and long situation? Do they always run a man-to-man defense against a short passing offense? Do they always slant to the wide side of the field? Do they always stay in the same pass coverage or do they vary it? What is my team likely to see when faced with third and long? What is their goal line defense? These are some of the questions that must be answered if an effective strategy is to be implemented for the next game.

It isn't enough that there are all these decisions to be made, but they have to be made the day after the last game and formulated into a game plan within two days so that the practices can be geared to perfecting the game plan.

STRATEGY TO BEAT THE DEFENSE

Offensively, the Seahawks first try to beat the opponent's basic defensive alignment, its theory of defense and its basic coverage. Does the team generally run a 4-3 or a 3-4? Do the linemen charge hard like the Bears or the Raiders, or do they play more of a hit and react technique such as the Rams and Patriots? Are they basically a man-to-man team, or are they a zone team like the Seahawks or the Patriots?

Next the Seahawks like to try to create a mismatch. In developing their passing strategy, they try to put their best receiver on the opponent's poorest defender. Or if the other team runs a lot of zone defense, the Seahawks might try to get two men into one defender's zone. If the other team plays a lot of man-to-man defense, the Seahawks might try to get their fastest receiver on the slowest defender, such as a running back against a linebacker.

In developing the running strategy, the Seahawks might try to create a mismatch by bringing their tight end to the side they want to run so that they can double team a tough defensive end. Or they might motion a slot back to help block at a certain hole. Maybe he could trap a lineman from the outside or perhaps help out on a double team. If a team plays a lot of zone defense and doesn't adjust well to strength when the Seahawks bring a man from one side of the field to the other, they might motion our flanker to the play side and thus gain an additional blocker.

There should be plans for at least two ways to block every problem defender. The Howie Longs and Lawrence Taylors of this league just can't be handled on every play with a one on one basic block. They have to be hit by different people, both linemen and backs, and they have to be double or triple teamed if a team expects its quarterback to survive until halftime.

Coach Hank Stram is known for his ability to scout personnel and come up with ways to beat certain individuals. He would look for the two or three best people, the ones he had to control to win, then devise ways to beat them. He didn't want a person or a team to be able to effectively do what they had been able to do best.

If a nose guard couldn't be handled one-on-one, the team might double team him. If he reacted well to the pressure, the team might block him into the hole and let him fight away from it with his excellent pursuing techniques. If a tackle was an aggressive rusher when he read pass, the team might run a draw trap.

Against a quick reacting linebacker, Stram's team might run play action passes to keep him out of his zone, or draws might go if he reacted back very quickly to the quarterback's drop. Against a great defensive back, his team might swing a back into his area or maybe the quarterback would look him off (look one way to get him anticipating a pass one way, then quickly throwing the other way).

Coaches also have to think about what their opponent's expect them to do. Because most teams scout themselves each game, they will know their tendencies as well as their opponents do. (Most self scouting reports usually cover the team's last four games and are about 110 pages long.)

Self scouting tells coaches what they have been likely to do in each situation. So if the Seahawks comes up with a third-and-three and have been running to Marcus most of the time, they might decide to throw deep, or let Marcus throw the running pass.

RUNNING GAME STRATEGY

First the coach must determine whether the opponent's running defense is based on a hit and pursue or an attacking and penetrating type of defense. Versus the strong pursuit type teams the offense might well think first of quick plays and counter plays. Versus the attacking defense the offense might think of using wide plays, especially the quick pitch, and trapping plays.

Next the coach has to look at the basic alignment used by the opponent's defense. How many down linemen does he use?—three, four, five, or six? Do they stay in that set or do they over- or under-shift often?

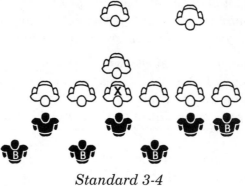

Standard 3-4

3-4 overshifted to the tight end side (linebackers undershifted)   *3-4 undershifted away from the tight end (backers overshifted)*

Does the opponent use multiple defensive sets? If so, which players have to learn more than one assignment?

Changed to 4-3 with one linebacker now playing a defensive tackle

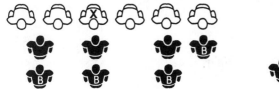

3-4 with stacked backers   *3-4 okie strong, eagle weak*

Does the team blitz or stunt? If so, when is it most likely to do so; on obvious passing downs, on long yardage, on short yardage, on first down? If the team stunts, who is most likely to stunt; a middle backer, an outside backer, a safety, a corner? Or do they prefer to twist the linemen when rushing a pass, keeping their backers free to pursue the run or drop for the pass? The 1985 Raiders had, at various times, used every defensive player in some sort of blitz or aggressive rush.

What are the keys of the linebackers? Do they seem to key the guards, the full-back, the halfback? If so, a false pull and a counter might work.

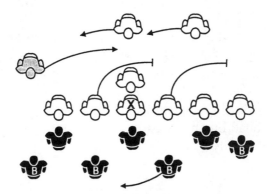

Wingback counter (if linebackers ignore the pull of the guards.)

Do the linemen try to fight through the head of the offensive blocker? (Defensive linemen who use a hit and react type of technique will generally use the blocker's head as the key as to which way the play is going. So if a blocker puts his head on my right side I can assume that the play is going to my right.) If so, you might try to false block him. That is have the blocker put his head away from the side you want to block him—then let him fight away from the play.

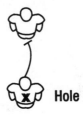

Normal shoulder block (head of blocker next to the hole)

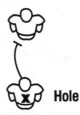

False block (blocker's head away from hole)

Another way to work on a good defensive lineman who reacts well is to influence him. In an influence block, one man false blocks a defender, then releases on a linebacker or defensive back. A trapper then comes to take the defender in the same way he is reacting. In the following diagram the offensive tackle influences the defensive tackle by putting his head on the outside, then slipping the block. Meanwhile the offside guard traps the tackle.

False block (influence) and trap

What is the action of the defensive backs? If they are a four deep team, do they get their run support mainly from the safeties or from the corners? Do they play a lot of man to man? If so, perhaps a wide run at a cornerback who is watching his man run deep, rather than watching for the run, might work.

The offensive strategist must look for weaknesses in the individual linemen and linebackers. Are there any injuries to the starters which must be filled by second stringers? Is one player adept at going to his right but not to his left, or is one player relatively slow? Does one linebacker react too slowly to a run, or does he commit so quickly that he might be vulnerable to a counter or to a special blocking technique?

DEVELOPING THE PASSING STRATEGY

Coaches always want the threat of the deep pass. If it's there—great! If not, it opens up other things, like 20 yard hooks or outs. And often those 20 yard patterns go all the way. Coaches may only call six or eight long passes in which the deep man is the prime receiver, but most teams have receivers going deep a lot when the quarterback isn't even paying attention to them. Of course, if they are open when they are decoys, the coach will soon call a play where they become the prime receivers.

When a coach expects a defensive line to hit and pursue on the run, he can expect a somewhat slower pass rush because the defender must first hit, then recognize the pass, then rush. This is slower than the defender who is aggressively attacking a gap. The 1985 Chicago Bears illustrate the hard charging type of defense which will get a good share of sacks. This makes it more difficult to get sufficient time for a complete passing attack.

In order to combat the hard charging linemen and the blitzing defenses, a coach might decide to just throw short. This is what Miami did in beating the "bad Bears" of 1985. Instead of having the quarterback drop seven steps he might just use the patterns which have one, three, or five step drops with quick releases. Or he might decide to sprint or roll away from the rush—assuming that he has a mobile quarterback.

Do the opponents always use a 4-3 or a 5-2 zone? Do they always use a tight man-for-man defense? If either of these is true the types of pass patterns which will work against man-to-man or zone can be put into the game plan.

Coaches must also account for every possible rusher on or near the line of scrimmage. They also have to have more than one way to block each man. If the defense is overloaded to one side, the coach must be able to slide his linemen over to pick up the possible rushers. Perhaps he will shift his tight end over to the defensive strong side. Or he needs to have a back ready to block to the side which the defense has overloaded.

On the goalline are the opponents always in a man-to-man defense? If so, crossing patterns, hooks, or fade patterns can be put into the game plan.

In creating the mismatch you might look for a weak defender against which you can put your best receiver. How can this best be accomplished? Perhaps he is a cornerback. If so, you can motion your best receiver toward him or flank your best receiver on his side.

Can you coax the defensive line to rush aggressively then run screens and draws? Or can you get outside the rush with a quick pitch or a swing pass?

Will the linebackers react to a run fake so that play action passes can be completed? Will defensive backs react up to a run fake so that a receiver can be sneaked deep on them for an easy touchdown?

DEVELOPING THE OVERALL STRATEGY FOR THE GAME

In preparing for a team, a coach has to think of the overall theories of the coach. What does he like to do? Is he conservative like Chuck Knox or is he a gambler like Don Coryell. If he has been in the league a long time we know a lot about him. But what about the new coach in the league? When a Dan Reaves, a Mike Ditka, or a Raymond Berry comes into the league we assume that he will have been influenced by Tom Landry, because they were all Cowboy assistants. We have to think about the new assistants, too. Which coaches have influenced them?

So a computer analysis might record a team's tendencies over several years to give an idea as to the coach's thinking on such concerns as: when does he like to block punts, How often does he use an on sides kick off, when is he likely to blitz, what types of plays does he like on third and long yardage, or what are his favorite goalline plays.

A team can't change its overall style every week and still be successful. Since the execution of the plays is of critical importance, new plays, pass patterns, defensive reads, or pass coverages can't be changed on a weekly basis. We may change something just a bit. Perhaps we will decide to run a pattern a few yards deeper or throw the halfback pass to a different player or from a different formation. It may be just enough to throw off the opponents but it isn't enough to take a lot of our practice time in perfecting it.

Teams are also concerned with how their upcoming opponents have played against a team which is similar to them in playing style? If their opponent is successful against the Bears, Seahawks, or New England , they might expect something similar to be tried against them.

A major part of most team's strategy for every game is "how can we get the big play?" On what situations are they likely to play man to man or to blitz? What are they likely to do on third down and short yardage?

Most coaches will call certain plays early in the game to see how the defense will adjust. The coach may look for defensive adjustments to stretch motion (running a back further out to the same side on which he started), to crossing motion (having the back go across the formation therefore changing formation strength), to a slot and flanker set, to an unbalanced line, to the reaction of the linebackers on a play action pass. And of course, the coach wants to know what they do in short yardage situations.

Years ago Sid Gilman got credit for using the first quarter to analyze the opponent's defense—then attacking that defense for the next three quarters. Many coaches have followed his lead.

Many coaches will attempt to beat the linebackers. By using draws and screens in passing situations and play action passes in running situations, they will try to fool the backers who have both run and pass responsibilities.

Another factor which might change a team's strategy is the injury factor. If a team's best passer or receiver is out of the game, the running attack might become more important in the game plan. If the best runner or pulling guard is hurt it might mean another type of change for the game plan.

The weather is another factor to consider. If the weather is expected to be very cold or wet, it might mean that the running game would become the dominant part of the game plan. Power plays, quick plays, or counters might have a better chance of working than long passes. Or perhaps the coach might decide to punt on early downs and wait for the opponents to make mistakes which would result in turnovers.

The opponent might be so strong that the only way possible to try to run on them would be with trick plays: reverses, counters, using an unbalanced line, giving them unusual formations, "Statue of Liberty" plays, etc. It might be that their strengths can be used against them.

THE OFFENSIVE GAME PLAN

Most coaches develop a Ready List of plays for each situation. Both the head coach, on the field, and the offensive coordinator, in the pressbox, will have copies of this list. Following is a sample of what a Ready List would look like.

DEVELOPING THE DEFENSIVE STRATEGY

As the first priority in the game, the Seahawks want to take away their oppenents' bread and butter plays, whether the play is the off tackle, the isolation series, or the short passing game. It is their goal to stop what the other team does best and get them to use their secondary attack.

READY LIST

VS. _____

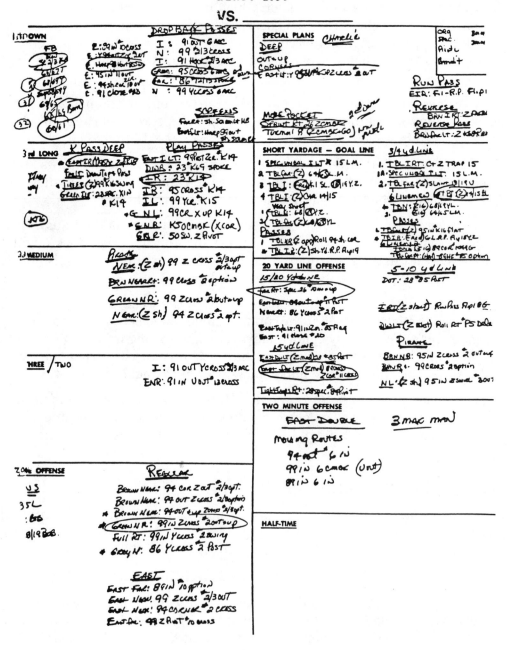

A ready list for a Super Bowl game

Secondly, the Seahawks want to know when they might get a big play. When are they likely to pass long or run a screen? If they can get a sack at this time, the other team will lose a lot of yardage and their down. Seattle and Phoenix work a great deal on getting the big defensive play.

The Seahawks look for the big defensive play, the sack, or the interception, when they have forced an obvious passing situation. In these situations, they may gamble in order to get the big play. You see, they look for that big play on both offense and defense. And when a team goes for the big play, they must gamble, but not as if they are in Las Vegas. A great team gambles when the odds are in their favor. If they are going to play the pass line, they want the dice to be loaded.

The Seahawks want to know how to get to the opponent's quarterback. Does he always drop back? Does he scramble a lot, usually to his right? Does he look for a hole in the middle to run through if his receivers are covered? The Seahawks will certainly prepare differently for a Testeverde or Marino than they will for a Montana or Young.

Against a team with one outstanding receiver, it might be determined to double cover him all the time, or perhaps only in certain passing situations. Or the Raiders might decide to just cover him with their best defender. Against a team with a good short passing attack, they might decide to go man-to-man a lot.

In looking at the scouting reports, one may find that a team has pet formations for favorite plays. Some teams will nearly always pass from a split back set. Or they may use their motion back extensively—using him to lead block or trap when he is near the offensive line, and using him as a prime receiver when he is wider. If so, he becomes a major key for the defense. Or they may ignore their back in motion, using him only to shift or spread the defense.

The scouting report may reveal that the team plays very conservatively inside its own 30. This means that the defense can become more aggressive and perhaps downplay the possibility of a pass. The report may show that the team favors running to its right or to the wide side of the field. This could signal the defensive coordinator to slant the line or stunt a linebacker into the expected flow of the play.

An analysis of the scouting report may suggest that a team's basic keys may not be too effective. If the defensive line has been taught to follow a pulling lineman but the upcoming opponent likes to pull one guard to influence the defender to follow him, then trap that defender—the defense might have to unlearn that key.

Perhaps the linebackers have been taught to key the guards, but the opponents never pull the guards or double team with them—so a better key might be found for that game.

Perhaps the defensive backs have been taught to key the offside tackle and end for a run or pass play but the tackle never releases immediately downfield, a new key may have to be found.

Some teams will keep their keys the same throughout the season, others will change somewhat from week to week to get the best possible defense for the upcoming opponents. Against a team that runs the I formation, the key may be the fullback, or read guard to fullback—which would have a better chance at stopping the countering game. Against a team which doesn't cross its backs the linebackers can key the near back, but if the backs cross, such as in a cross buck, it would be necessary to key the opposite back.

Sometimes the scouts will pick up a cheat which can be exploited by the defense. A fullback might line up closer than normal on cross bucks or when he is expected to pass block. Or maybe a flanker will line up closer to the center if he is going to run a reverse. Or a tight end might cheat out a bit when he is going to release for a pass.

Some years ago Coach Red Sanders' scouts picked up a key on Stanford quarterback John Brodie. Whenever he was going to hand off for a run he lined up with his feet close together and his toes parallel to the line of scrimmage, but when he was going to pass he had his right foot back. Whenever the Bruins spotted Brodie's feet staggered they would yell "Omaha" which signalled them to rush eight men. The result was a good number of sacks and a 72-0 victory for U.C.L.A.—avenging the 21 to 18 loss the year before.

Sometimes there will be a key that can signal the linebackers which way the play will probably go. A quarterback may always use an open pivot—opening up towards the flow of the quick or power plays or the fullback may always lead the tailback. If this is so, the defensive coordinator can start the linebackers toward the flow quickly—leaving only the necessary people on the offside to defend against a countering action or reverse. Often this key can be combined with another key which will stop the counters. If the counters always come from a wingback some defenders can key him and yell "reverse" when he starts opposite the flow.

Perhaps you can shake up the offense with a change of pace or something which they hadn't seen before. In the 1985 Citrus Bowl game, Ohio State started rushing Robbie Bosco of BYU with only two men while dropping back 9. This confused BYU. As BYU began to make adjustments Ohio State began rushing three, four or more and blitzing others. The strategy was highly effective in that BYU scored only one touchdown in their 10 to 7 defeat.

KICKING GAME STRATEGY

The kicking game is a highly scouted aspect of football. It is an area in which many breaks can be made, especially if they are planned.

The average distance of their kicks, their hang time, the type of kick coverage, and the speed of the kick off team are among the things which are considered when the other team is kicking off. If the kick off is generally short a team may emphasize the return that week. If the kicking team coverage stays in lanes like they are supposed to (about 3 to 5 yards apart) a middle return will probably work best. If they converge quickly on the ball, a wide return will be best. If most of them converge but those responsible for the wide plays stay wide, then a trap return will probably work best. If the kicking team crosses their widest men to make it more difficult to trap, that has to be taken into consideration in setting up the blocking rules.

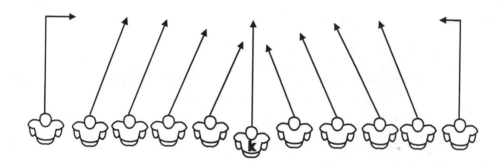

Kick off team converging with ends staying wide

When kicking, a team must consider the best return man for the opponents and kick away from him. The coach must know if they are likely to wedge, cross block, or trap in order to prepare our coverage people for blocks from the side or the power of the wedge from the front.

If the other team peels back quickly on the kick off, the coach might consider an onsides kick. In the 1966 Rose Bowl, UCLA pulled off what might have been the biggest upset in this traditional game. Top ranked, undefeated Michigan State was favored by two touchdowns. After a fumbled punt, UCLA scored. They kicked onsides and recovered, then quickly marched 42 yards to score. The Bruins got all of their 14 points without the Spartans touching the ball. Then they held on to win 14-12. Tommy Prothro, the UCLA coach, was a championship bridge player as well as a highly successful coach. His strategic and tactical decisions won a good many games for him—at the card table and on the gridiron.

When the other team is punting, the coach must know how many seconds it takes for the center to snap the ball to the kicker and how long it takes the kicker to get the ball off. Does he take long steps? Is the center likely to snap high or on the ground? If so, the team can work on a block.

Many teams will always put a man on the center to hit him as he snaps. If you can get him to start thinking about taking the hit instead of making the snap, you may be able to get a bad snap out of him. Or he may snap extra hard so that he can quickly set himself to protect from the hit he knows he will receive. This also makes it more likely that he will snap high.

We will have to decide where the block should occur. We might aim 5 yards from where the kicker lined up or we might be able to aim closer to the punter—if he takes short steps.

Next the coach will have to determine where to attempt the block. Is their spacing between linemen such that we might be able to block from the outside. Or can we create a gap inside and stunt through it?

The punting team wants to make certain that they get the punt off. But if a team never rushes the kicker, the coach might think of having the punter hold the ball for a second before he kicks it—in order to give the coverage people a chance to get further downfield. If they hit and peal back to set up a return, it might be wise to fake the punt and pass or run. If they always rush the punter, the fake punt might work. Should the coach decide to use a fake, maybe a pass into the area from which their rush had come would work.

Most punt return teams don't make any changes. However, if the other team has had a personnel change, it might affect who and how the team would double team to slow up their punt coverage.

While most teams wouldn't plan on anything different in their field goal attempt, they might change their fake field goal play depending on the expected coverage by the defense.

The field goal block might be changed if a team found that one of the blockers generally created a gap. If the oppenents always blocked a man on his outside, they might put a man on his outside then stunt a man through the gap created. If their end always blocked down and their wingback always took the outside responsibility, they might put a man on the end charging down and a man on the back charging outside, then stunt a man between them.

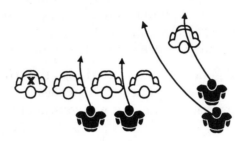

Stunt to block field goal or extra point

THE CHALLENGE OF MAKING THE STRATEGIC DECISIONS

Some teams stay very basic with their offense and defense. Their idea is to mini-mize their own mistakes. Other teams look for technical advantages and change somewhat from week to week in their attack and defense.

Sometimes the strategy hinges on pre-game publicity. In 1904, Coach Fielding Yost at Michigan publicized the fact that his 265 pound lineman, Babe Carter, (the original "ice box") would carry the ball near the goalline. In the game he inserted Carter as a back when his team got near the goalline. Carter faked, and another back scored.

The hype of the 1986 Super Bowl had us all wondering. Would Eason be able to play even though he had the flu? Or would Grogan start? Would McMahon be able to play with his sore buttock or would his acupuncturist have to start the game? A defense prepares somewhat differently depending on which quarterback might start, so the supposed pre-game indecision by one coach might result in a lot of headaches for his opponent.

Before their playoff game meeting in 1986, John Robinson of the Rams said that Dallas often added plays if there was a strategic reason for it, but that the Rams were not inclined to do anything different from week to week. Then in the game it was the Rams who had all the new plays.

. When Mike Ditka unleashed "The Refrigerator," opposing coaches had to give some thought to defending him. Each week Ditka put in a new wrinkle for The Fridge. One week he led the ball carrier at the goalline. The next week he carried the ball. The next week, in an unplanned tactic, he carried the ball carrier over the goal. The next week he caught a pass. The Frige was not really such a major factor, but he did have to be considered in the plans of the defense.

Prior to The Fridge with the Bears, Bill Walsh had used a lineman in the backfield on certain plays. Walsh could always be depended on to come up with a new formation, an unbalanced line or some other gimmick. It caused many teams problems in preparation and adjustments. Gimmicks don't necessarily make for a successful season. Many successful offensive teams seldom use major change ups. The Raiders, Bears, Patriots, and Seahawks are among the teams that stay pretty basic.

The coaching staff will generally see more things that they can do than the team will have time to practice. The major question is whether the time spent in teaching the changes in offense, defense, or kicking will gain more than just practicing the basic plays and defenses.

For many coaches, the week to week strategic adjustments are the most interesting and challenging aspects of the season. This is a major factor in the violent chess match of football.

12

How to Watch the Game

When watching football, most fans just watch the ball. As most of the excitement generally is somewhere around the ball, this is not necessarily a bad idea. However, because there are generally six individual battles going on at the line of scrimmage and at least two or three other battles going on in the defensive secondary, there is really more going on than any one person can see at any time. This is why coaches must go over a single play hundreds of times in the film room the day after the game. However, there are a few simple tricks that will enable the football fan to see far more on any one play than the average spectator is able to comprehend.

Television viewing generally limits your options for viewing, especially on kicking and passing downs because the camera generally follows the ball. On kicking downs, the camera follows the ball as it sails 40 yards above the field. The fans at home are not shown the multiple clashes involving the return plays and kick coverage going happening on the field.

On passing plays, the camera focuses on the quarterback so that the fan can see some of the individual pass blocking and pass rush battles that occur near the quarterback, but the camera misses seeing the overall pass pattern develop.

Whether you are watching from a stadium seat or your living room sofa, you should always watch the interior line as the ball is snapped. The guards are particularly good keys for most teams.

1. If the guard blocks aggressively on a defensive lineman, it is probably a running play. However, it could be a play action pass.

2. If the guard blocks a linebacker, there is an even greater certainty that it is a run, although recent rules allow for linemen to release downfield if the pass is caught behind the line of scrimmage. Therefore, there is a small possibility that the play is a screen pass.

3. If the guard drops back in pass protection, it will probably be a pass or draw play.

4. If the guard pulls behind the line of scrimmage, he is generally leading the play. So the play may be a trap or a wide power play.

Sometimes a tackle or the center will pull or trap. If you start watching the play with your eyes on the guards, you will be able to see any actions of the linemen, and you will have an immediate clue to the type of play which is about to develop. It will only take one to two tenths of a second to recognize the type of play. You can then decide whether to continue watching the "real game" in the line or switch to watching the ball carrier or the passer.

The television camera is limited by what the director wants us to see. He normally opts to show us close-ups rather than the totality of the game. Consequently, it is always better to watch the game in person.

In choosing your seat for a game, there are several things to think about. Many fans like to sit on the 50-yard line. With a seat on the 50, you are closest to the action, and you can more easily see the depth of the game (the distance of a run or the depth of a pass). However, many coaches prefer to watch the game from high in the end zone, and even if there are no end zone seats, they will get as high in the stands and as far from the 50 as possible.

The advantage of sitting high in the end zone is that you can see more of the adjustments that the teams are making. From the end zone, you can see the split of the offensive linemen and the shades of the defensive linemen, as well as the pulls, traps, and the double teams of the offensive line. It is also easier to see the twists and stunts of the defensive linemen and backers and whether or not the defensive backs are taking away the inside or the outside patterns by their alignments. From above, you can see the total offensive pass pattern unfolding, so you can better second guess the passer by reading the defense.

The disadvantages of watching from the end zone relate almost entirely to the lack of depth perception. You can't tell how far a ball carrier has to run. You can never second guess the officials on whether or not a first down has been made, and you can't tell how far a kick or a pass traveled.

Once you have chosen your seat, you can decide on whether to watch as much of the game as possible or just to concentrate on one aspect, such as the passing attack and pass defense or the line play. Some people like to zero in on just one part of the game. Perhaps when the Dolphins and Dan Marino are in town, you might decide to concentrate on the line play and see how the techniques have changed since you played. Or if Buddy Ryan is in town, you might want to focus on his defensive tactics.

Assuming that you want to see as much of the whole game as possible, you should start with the linemen. If the linemen run, you should look for the ball carrier. If the linemen pass, you might look immediately downfield to see how the pattern is developing. You might miss the sacks, but you'll see a lot more of the strategies of the opposing coaches.

Watching the substitutions made can give you another hint as to a coach's technical plans. Is the nickel back coming into the game? Is a second tight end being substituted?

WATCHING THE INDIVIDUAL BATTLES

The real battles are in the line. If you want to watch some of these battles focus first on a blocker. How does he block? Does he charge hard with his shoulder into the man on him? Does he drive with his hands into the defender's chest and drive him? Or does he drop back and set for a pass block?

The run blocks can be an aggressive shoulder block, used when a defender must be moved, as when he is on the goal line, or a drive block using the hands to make contact with the defender's chest. This type of block allows the blocker to stay in contact with the defender longer. Because the rules have changed to allow for blocking the hands, this technique has been used frequently. Initially it was legal only for pass protection, but now it is legal in run blocking plays as well.

In this technique, the blocker drives his hands into his defender's chest and tries to "grab cloth." He then drives his legs in an attempt to straighten up the defender and move him backward. If he is able to control the defender, he straightens him up and then explodes his arms upward knocking the defender backwards and "decleating" him (knocking him off his cleats). This doesn't happen often unless the blocker is exceptional in technique and strength. Former U.S.C. player Dave Cadigan had more than 30 "decleaters" in one game. If records were kept of this very important play, it would certainly have been the one to beat.

Meanwhile the defender is hitting into the blocker and keeping him away from his body while reacting to his assignments, usually trying to move across the blocker's face to the ball. In a hit and react type of defense, the best key as to where the ball is going is to move opposite to the force of the block. As the blocker will generally put his head to the side of the defender (which will protect the hole), the defender must move through the head, across the face, of the blocker. If the defender takes the easy way and runs around behind the blocker, the ball would already be ahead of him so he would have no chance to make the play.

As we mentioned, the offensive lineman is trying to "grab cloth" on the front of the defender's jersey. The defender is trying to the same thing to the blocker. While this is technically illegal, it is certainly executed often. Normally the officials will call a penalty only when the hold is wider than the chest. Many sports allow for actions which are technically illegal but have become part of the game. Hand checking in basketball and the underwater tactics used by water polo players are examples of "legal-illegal" plays.

Naturally, the players don't like to be held so they take special measures to reduce the chances that they will be. Some players sew velcro on the inside of the jersey in the chest and shoulder areas. Some will use double sided adhesive tape to stick the jersey to the shoulder and rib pads. Some equipment men order jerseys several sizes smaller than the player normally wears. It may take three men and a boy with a large shoe horn to get the players into these undersized shirts, and they may be uncomfortable, but it is impossible to grip the fabric of the player's jersey.

WATCHING THE PASS BLOCKING AND PASS RUSH

On passes, the blockers will generally take a step back and to the inside. They set up with their feet wide and their weight balanced. Their arms will be held in front of the chest with the elbows down. When the pass rusher comes at the blocker, he will punch into the rusher's chest with both hands so that the palms of the blocker's hands will be flat against the front of the rusher's shoulder pads. He will punch and recoil. If the blocker were to leave his hands on the rusher, the rusher would grab one of the blocker's arms and gain control of the battle, so the blocker must recoil quickly and then punch again. He does this while quickly moving his feet so that he can stay in front of the rusher.

The blocker will also have some special assignments. See if you can pick up what that assignment is on each play. The most common blocking scheme is man-to-man, usually referred to as "big-on-big." If the defense is in a four man line, the offensive guards will take the defensive tackles (who are already aligned on them), and the offensive tackles will take the defensive ends (who have lined up on them). A problem occurs when the tackles twist, the tackle and the end twist, or the defensive lineman slants in and out and a linebacker cross charges. If the assignment is man-to-man and there is a defensive stunt, the blocker assigned to the defender who is moving must step behind his teammate and pick up the pass rusher after he has completed his stunt. This skill is difficult to learn and makes man-to-man protection less effective when the defense stunts a lot.

Another type of protection is called zone protection. Here the blocker steps back and takes whoever comes to him. This is often more effective against stunting teams.

Yet another type of protection is called slide protection. Sometimes one player is so dominating that the offense will slide an extra man over to help in the pass.

When you are watching a great pass rusher, especially a defensive end, watch how the offense makes blocking adjustments to control him. Do they put two linemen on him, do they use a lineman and a back, or do they try to slow him up by running play action passes or screen?

The other part of the pass rush battle is the rusher's techniques. While the blocker is retreating slowly and punching quickly into the rusher's chest, the rusher has several techniques that he can use. If the blocker has too much weight forward, the rusher can grab him and pull him forward (this is called the jerk). If the blocker has too much weight back, the defender can "bull rush" right over him and knock him down.

Most defensive moves involve going to one side or the other. It can start with a head fake or a head and body fake. The rusher may get the blocker moving one way then use one of several techniques to go the other way. A common technique is the club and swim. The defender can grab the wrist or the upper arm of the blocker (clubbing) and then "swim" over the blocker's shoulder with the other arm. This is a good technique for taller players. Shorter rushers may use the rip and run in which they drive the inside arm under the outside arm of the blocker, run through the blocker while lifting his shoulder and keeping him off-balance. Another technique is the spin. The defender starts one way and then spins away from his original direction and charges through the other side of the blocker. Some teams, even at the professional level, work on only one technique all season. As you can imagine, if you work on only one technique for 20 minutes a day for six months, you will become pretty good at it. Other teams work on several techniques and may use them in combination with two or three different rushes on each pass play.

One of the greatest challenges in football is that no matter what play your team runs, there is a counter for it. This is true not only for strategies and tactics but also for individual techniques as well. So the blocker has techniques which he can use to counter the different rushes of the defender.

If the rusher attempts to club or grab him, the blocker must quickly recoil his arm. Even if the rusher still has a hold, his hand will be farther from his shoulders so he will have less leverage. If the defender starts to swim over him with his arm high, the blocker can punch him under the arm with his free hand. At the same time, the blocker will move to cut off the path chosen by the rusher. If he keeps his elbows inside of his shoulders, he can usually prevent the rip and run. If the rusher tries to spin, the blocker must stay in front of the rusher and punch him with his palms as he spins.

WATCHING THE PASS RECEIVERS AND DEFENSIVE BACKS

While it takes a dedicated football fanatic (or an old lineman) to enjoy the battles at the line of scrimmage, lots of people enjoy watching a pass pattern develop. If you are at a game and are sitting in the end zone, you can see the developing pass play much better than if you are watching the game at home. The television cameras limit the view to the area near the ball, so it is difficult to see this action from the living room sofa.

Before the snap, see if you can get a pre-snap read, just as the quarterback and the receivers are trying to get one. Some teams try to keep all of their defenders in the same areas before the snap then move into their responsibilities after the play is underway. Other teams will move their defensive backs up or back, in or out, so they will be in the best position to carry out their jobs.

Are the defenders up at the line ready to bump and run? If so, watch the escape techniques the receiver has to use to get free. Does he head fake, double fake, or rip his arm up and through the defender's arm?

Do the defenders stay with the receivers closest to them or do they move into an zone? How does the receiver react to the movement of the defensive back? If it is a zone, which is played most of the time, he will have an area to move into. He may get open and then stop, or he may continue to run through an area getting more depth or width. If it is man-to-man, he should use double cut patterns like an "out and up " (chair), hook and go, or post-corner, or he can try to fake and run away such as in a hook or an out.

As the play develops, look for the areas where the receivers have gone. Are they pretty much in line (one deep, one about 15 to 20 yards, and one short)? Are they working on a vertical stretch of defense? Or, are they across the field in a horizontal stretch attempting to go between the linebackers?

There is so much to see in a football game. You can watch with the technical interest of a pro coach, or you can sit back with your drink and hot dogs and watch the ball and the band. Whichever you choose, you are ensured a couple of enjoyable hours with the game.

GLOSSARY

Angle block: Blocking a player inside or outside who is not "on" or "shading" the blocker.

Arc block: A block on the defensive end or corner by a running back with the back attempting to block the defender in. The blocker starts wide for a few steps then attacks the defender.

Audible: Changing the offensive play at the line of scrimmage.

Backpedal: Running directly backward, a technique used by defensive backs and linebackers.

Blitz: A defensive play in which a linebacker or defensive back attacks past the LOS.

Bomb: A long pass.

Boot or bootleg: Quarterback fakes to backs going one way while he goes the opposite way to run or pass

Bump and run: A technique in which the defensive back hits the potential receiver on the line of scrimmage then (to slow his route) then runs with the receiver.

Chucking: Hitting a receiver before the pass is thrown.

Clip: A block in which the defender is hit from behind. It is illegal unless done in the legal clipping zone, close to the snapper (two to five yards from the ball, depending on the level of play.)

Cloud: A commonly used term which indicates that the cornerback will cover the outside flat zone on a pass.

Combo or combination block: A block in which linemen exchange responsibilities.

Corners or corner backs: The widest secondary players in an umbrella (4 deep) defense.

Counter: A play which ends going a different direction than the initial flow of the backs would indicate.

Crackback block: A block by an offensive player who has lined up more than two yards outside of the tackle and is blocking low on a man inside him. It is illegal.

Crossover step: A step by a lineman or back in which, when moving laterally, the player steps first with the foot away from the direction toward which he is traveling.

Curl: A pass pattern in which the receiver runs 15 to 20 yards downfield then comes back toward the passer in an open area of the defensive coverage.

Cut back: The movement of a ball carrier away from the direction he was originally running so that he can run behind the tacklers.

Cut block: A block aimed at the ankles or knees of the defender. It is illegal at some levels of play.

Cut off: A block in which a player blocks a player who is closer to the hole than is the offensive player.

Dash: A planned passing action in which the passer drops back then moves to his right or left in a planned action. The blockers move with him.

Defense: The team which is not in control of the ball.

Dime defense: A defense in which six defensive backs are in the game in order to stop a likely pass.

Dive: A quick straight ahead play with the halfback carrying the ball.

Dog or red dog: A linebacker attacking past the LOS at the snap of the ball.

Double cover: Two defenders covering one offensive receiver.

Double team: A block in which two offensive players block one defender.

Down: A play which begins after the ball is stopped. There are two types of downs, a scrimmage down and a free kick down.

Down block: Linemen block down towards center.

Down lineman: A defensive lineman.

Drag: A delayed pattern in which a tight end or a wideout runs a shallow pattern across the center.

Draw: A fake pass which ends with one of the backs carrying the ball after the defensive linemen are "drawn" in on the pass rush.

Drive block: A straight ahead block.

Drop: The action of the passer as he moves away from the line of scrimmage. Three, five, seven and nine step drops are common.

Eagle: A 5-2 defensive alignment with the tackles outside of the offensive guards and the linebackers on the ends.

Encroachment: Entering the neutral zone (the line of scrimmage bounded by both ends of the ball) before the ball is snapped. It is a penalty in high school football. At the college and pro level it is a penalty only if contact is made with the other team.

End around: A reverse play in which a tight end or a wide out carries the ball.

End zone: The ten yard area between the goal line and the end line.

Even defense: A defensive alignment in which there is no defensive lineman over the center.

Extra point: See "point after touchdown."

Fade: A pass pattern used generally against a man-to-man coverage in which the receiver runs deep and fades away from the defender.

Fair catch: The opportunity for a receiving player to catch a kicked ball and not be tackled. It is signaled by waving one arm overhead. The ball cannot be advanced after making a fair catch. The team has an opportunity to put the ball in play by a scrimmage down or a free kick down.

False block: Hitting an opposing lineman on the same side as you wish him to move, used against good reacting defensive lineman.

Far: A player who is aligned away from where the ball will be run or passed. The "far" guard may trap block or the "far" back may be the ball carrier.

Field goal: A ball place kicked or drop kicked over the goal posts. It scores three points.

Flanker: A back split wider than a wingback.

Flipper: A forearm shiver.

Flood: A pass pattern in which the offense sends more receivers into an area than there are defenders. It uses both a horizontal and a vertical stretch.

Flow: The apparent direction of the ball during a scrimmage play. Most plays attack in the direction of the flow. Counters, reverses, and throwback passes go against the flow.

Fold: A block in which an offensive lineman blocks the next defender on the line while the offensive lineman nearest that defender moves behind the blocker and blocks the near backer.

Forearm shiver (lift or rip): A block protection technique in which the defender wards off the blocker by hitting and lifting him with his forearm.

Formation: The alignment of the offensive team. At least seven players must be within a foot of the line of scrimmage.

Forward pass: A pass thrown forward from behind the line of . scrimmage. College and pro teams are allowed only one forward pass per play. High schools are allowed multiple forward passes on one play.

Free kick down: A down in which the kicking team can tee up the ball to kick (as in a kick off) or can place kick or punt the ball after a safety. The defensive team must stay at least ten yards from the ball. Free kick downs occur after a touchdown or field goal. They can also occur after a safety (when the team scored against can have one scrimmage down or a free kick down in which it can kick the ball in any manner) or after a fair catch (in which the receiving team has the choice of a set of scrimmage downs or one free kick down in which it can score a field goal).

Free safety: The safety man opposite the power side of the offensive line (the tight end). He is usually free to cover deep zones.

Freeze option: A play in which an inside fake to one back running up the middle should freeze the linebackers. The play ends as an option play between the quarterback and another runner.

Front: The alignment of the defensive linemen.

Game plan: The offensive, defensive, and kicking strategy for an opponent.

Gap: The space between offensive or defensive linemen.

Gap defense: A defensive front with the defensive linemen in the offensive gaps.

Goal line: The area over the inside edge of the chalk mark which marks the end of the playing field. The ten yard end zone is beyond the goal line.

Guards: The offensive linemen on either side of the center.

Hand shiver: A defensive block protection in which the defender hits the blocker with his hands and extends his arms to keep the blocker away from his body.

Hang time: The amount of time a kick stays in the air.

Hash marks: Short lines parallel with the sidelines which intersect each five yard mark on the field. They are 1/3 of the way in from the sideline (18 2/3 yards) for high school and college and even with the goal posts for the pro game. Every play starts from a point on or between the hash marks

Hitch: A quick pattern to a wide receiver in which he drives off the line then stops.

Hitting position: A balanced "ready position" in which the weight is on the balls of the feet, the knees are flexed, the torso is flexed forward, and the head is up.

Hook block: A block in which the offensive blocker must get outside of a defender who is outside of him, then block that defender in.

Hook pattern: A pass pattern in which the receiver runs downfield, stops, then comes back toward the passer.

Horizontal stretch: Forcing the pass defenders to cover the entire width of the field on a pass.

Hot receiver: A receiver who becomes open because the defender who would have covered him has stunted into the offensive backfield. The receiver yells "hot" when he sees he will be open and the passer passes quickly to him.

I formation: A formation in which the quarterback, fullback, and tailback are in a line.

Influence: Getting an opponent to move in the direction desired through finesse.

Inside slot: A slot back aligned close to the tight lineman.

Invert: A four deep defensive alignment in which the safeties are closer to the LOS than the corners. They are expected to quickly assist in run support.

Jam: Hitting a potential receiver before the ball is released by the passer.

Key: Watching an opponent to determine what he or his team will be doing.

Lateral pass: A pass thrown parallel with the LOS or backward. It can be thrown overhand or underhand.

Lead: An offensive player goes through the hole and leads the ball carrier, usually looking to the inside to pick up a backer.

Lead step: A step with the foot closest to the direction toward which the player is moving.

Line of scrimmage: An area approximately a foot wide (the width of the ball) which stretches from sideline to sideline.

Load: A block in which an offensive player coming from the inside blocks a wide defender on a wide play. The blocker will have his head and shoulders on the offensive side of the defender and the play is designed to go around him.

Loop: A defensive lineman's move from a gap to a man, a man to a gap, or sometimes from a man to another man.

LOS: Line of scrimmage.

M4M: An abbreviation for man-for-man pass defense.

Mac: Middle linebacker (mac means "middle back").

Mike: Middle guard or "nose man" (Mike means "middle in").

Misdirection: A play which goes against the flow of the play, such as a bootleg, reverse, or throwback.

Muff: A mistake in catching the ball on a kicking play.

Near: The player aligned close to the point of attack. So the "near" guard may trap or the near back may be the ball carrier.

Neutral zone: The area bounded by each end of the ball which extends from sideline to sideline and from the ground to the sky. Only the snapper can be in that zone before the ball is snapped.

Nickel defense: A defense with five defensive backs.

Nose guard or nose tackle: A defensive lineman playing on the offensive center.

Odd defense: A defense which has a man on the offensive snapper. This will result in a defensive line with an odd number of players on it.

Offside: Side of the line away from where the play will attack.

Off tackle play: A play which hits in the area of the offensive tackle and end.

Offense: The team controlling the ball.

Okie: The Oklahoma 5-2 defense (Linebackers over the offensive guards).

On side: Side of the line to which the play will attack.

On side kick: A short kickoff which travels at least ten yards which can then be recovered by either team.

Option play: A play in which the quarterback runs at a wide defender forcing the defender to either tackle him or stop the pitch to a trailing back. QB can keep or pitch.

Overshift: The alignment of the defensive linemen one man closer to the strength of the formation.

Pass pattern: The path or route that a receiver runs in attempting to get open.

Passing tree: The potential routes which a receiver can run. When drawn together they resemble a tree.

Penetration: The movement across the line of scrimmage by the defenders.

Pick: A pass pattern in which one of the potential receivers hits or screens off a defender allowing his teammate to be free. It is used primarily against a man to man defense. It is illegal to hit a defensive back before the ball is caught but it is legal to create a screen by stopping (as in a hook pattern) or having the receivers cross close to each other.

Place kick: A kick in which the ball is either held by a player or held by a tee. It is used for kickoffs, field goals, and points after touchdowns.

Play action: A pass off of a run fake

Pocket: The area surrounding a passer which is being protected by his blockers.

Point after touchdown (P.A.T.): An extra play allowed after a touchdown in which the team has an opportunity to make one point by kicking the ball through over the goal posts or two points by running or passing the ball over the goal line (high school and college game only). Ball is spotted at the three yard line for this play.

Pre-snap read: A cue read by the quarterback or receivers based on the alignment of the pass defenders.

Prevent defense: A defense sometimes used by a team which is ahead late in a half. It uses extra defensive backs playing deeper than usual and fewer than normal pass rushers.

Primary receiver: The first choice of the passer in a pass pattern.

Pull: The movement of an offensive lineman behind the line as he leads the play.

Punt: A kick made on a scrimmage down which is designed to make the most yardage when possession is changed.

Pursuit: The movement of the defensive players to get them to a spot where they can make the tackle.

Quick count: A snap count which gets the ball in play quicker than normal, hoping to catch the defensive team unprepared.

Quick side: The side of the offensive line away from the strong side.

Reach block: An offensive lineman blocking a defender who is closer to the point of attack than himself or a tight end getting outside position on a backer who is slightly outside of him.

Read: Getting an idea of what the opponents are doing by looking at one or more of them as the play develops. It can be done by defenders watching offensive linemen or backs or by passers and receivers watching pass coverage defenders.

Reduced front: A defensive lineman playing closer to the center than normal. An example would be a tackle playing on the guard rather than on the offensive tackle.

Release: The movement of a receiver in leaving the line of scrimmage.

Reverse: A play in which a wide player on one side runs the ball against the flow of the other backs.

Rollout: A deep, generally wide, path of the quarterback behind the other backs.

Rove: See dash.

Rover: A defensive back who can be given various assignments. He is usually playing in a defense which has a 5-2 front and three defensive backs.

Run force: The responsibility of a defender to make the runner commit to an inside or outside path once he has passed the offensive end.

Sack: The tackling of the passer before he has a chance to pass.

Safety: A two-point play which occurs when an offensive player is tackled behind his own end zone.

Safetyman: The defensive back or backs with the deepest responsibility.

Scoop: A block in which a lineman blocks the next defensive man to the play side this releases the next lineman out to block a backer.

Scramble: The running of the quarterback after he has been forced out of the pocket on a pass play.

Scrape: The path of a linebacker who is moving into the offensive line—usually on a key.

Screen: A pass, usually behind the LOS, after a deep drop by the quarterback. Some linemen pull to lead the receiver.

Scrimmage down: One of four attempts of the offense to advance the ball ten yards and make another first down.

Seams: The areas between the defensive zones which are more likely to be open to complete passes.

Secondary: The safetymen and cornerbacks.

Set: The offensive or defensive alignment.

Set up: The last step of a quarterback's drop—the spot from which he would like to pass.

Shading: The defender is not head up on the blocker but part of his body overlaps the body of the offensive player.

Shift: A change of alignment from one set to another before the snap of the ball. It can be used by the offensive or the defensive team.

Shiver: A defensive technique used to protect the defender from the block. It can be done with the hands or the forearms contacting the blocker.

Short list: The list of plays most likely to be used in a game with plays listed according to each situation.

Shotgun: A formation in which the quarterback sets several yards behind the center to be able to see the field better on a pass play. More wide receivers are also used. Some runs will be made from this formation to keep the defense honest.

Shuffle: The path of a linebacker who is moving nearly parallel with the LOS as he diagnoses the play and determines how he will attack the ball carrier.

Signals: Offensive or defensive code words which tell the team which alignment and which play to use. Also the cadence called by the quarterback to get the play started.

Sky: A term used in pass coverage to indicate that a safety will cover a short flat zone.

Slant: As a defensive lineman it is a hard move usually from an offensive lineman into a gap, as an offensive term it is a pass pattern, usually by a wide receiver, angling in toward the center of the field.

Slip block: Same as scoop.

Slot: A back lined up in the area between a split end and the tackle.

Snap: The act of putting the ball in play. It can be handed to the quarterback or thrown (between the legs or to the side) to a back.

Snapper: The offensive lineman who puts the ball in play, usually the center.

Spearing: An illegal action in which a player drives his head into a player, usually a player on the ground.

Speed option: An option play in which there is no inside fake. All backs run wide immediately.

Sprint draw: A draw play off of a sprint out move by the quarterback.

Sprint out: A fast and shallow path of the quarterback

Spy: Keeping a defender near the line of scrimmage on pass plays in order to stop a draw play or a run by the quarterback.

Squib kick: A low flat kickoff which is difficult to handle. It is often used when the receiving team has an effective kick returner or when the kicking team does not have a long ball kicker.

Stack: Playing a linebacker directly behind a defensive lineman.

Streak: A pass pattern in which the receiver runs long and fast.

Stretch: To widen the defense by placing offensive men in wide positions.

Strong safety: The safety on the strong side (tight end) of the offense.

Strong side: The side of the offensive line which blocks for the power plays. Usually the side of the tight end is designated the strong side.

Stunt: A defensive maneuver in which linemen create a hole for a backer to move through the line or a movement between defensive linemen which will allow at least one to penetrate the LOS.

Sweep: A wide offensive power running play.

Tight end: A receiver playing close to the offensive tackle.

Touchback: A play which ends behind the receiver's goal line but in which the impetus of the ball was generated by the other team. There is no score. The ball is moved to the 20 yard line for the first down.

Trap: Blocking a defensive lineman by an offensive player who did not line up close to him originally. In a trap block the blocker will have his head on the defensive (downfield) side of the opponent and the play is designed to go inside the block.

Triangle: Triple key for a defensive player. A blocking triangle involves the three most dangerous blockers who could attack him. For a linebacker it would involve one or two linemen and one or two backs.

Twist: A movement between defensive linemen, especially in a pass situation, in which the linemen cross hoping that at least one will get clear into the backfield.

Two minute offense: The attack used by a team late in a half when they are behind and attempting to score while conserving time.

Umbrella: A secondary four deep alignment usually with the corners closer to the LOS than the safeties.

Unbalanced line: An offensive alignment in which four or more linemen are set on one side of the line of scrimmage.

Undershift: A defensive alignment in which the defensive linemen have moved a man away from their normal position away from the strength of the offensive formation.

Uprights: The vertical poles which hold up the cross bar of the goal posts.

Vertical stretch: Forcing the pass defenders to cover deep even if the pass is in the short or intermediate zones.

Waggle: A pass action off a running play in which the quarterback moves wide and deep after faking to a back. Some coaches call it a waggle if the quarterback move in the direction of the flow behind the backs to whom he has faked. Others call it a waggle if he moves opposite the flow and is protected by a pulling lineman.

Walkaway: A position taken by a linebacker or defensive back between a wide receiver and the offensive linemen. It allows the defender to be in position to stop the quick slant pass and still be able to play a wide run.

Weak side: The side of the offense away from the tight end.

Wedge: A block in which three or more players block an area.

Wide out: A split end or flanker.

Wide receiver: See wide out.

Wing: A back lined up outside a tight end (usually a yard outside and a yard back).

Zone blocking: Pass protection blockers protect an area rather than blocking a specific man. It is used against stunting defenses.

Zone defense: A pass coverage in which the linebackers and defensive backs protect areas and play the ball rather than watch specific men.

A FINAL WORD

Those of us who coach obviously have a great passion for the game of football. Part of its charm comes from the camaraderie with the coaching staff and players. Some comes from the development of new theories of offense and defense that are revamped during the off-season, but the primary reason for the fascination of football is in the weekly challenges of the games, the violent chess match.

It is the intellectual side of football, which so many people have failed to comprehend, that makes the game exciting. So many spectators see only the crunching of bodies or the acrobatics of the ball carriers. We hope that this book has disclosed some ideas that will help the reader to appreciate the great game and its masters just a little bit more.